# Legacies of Faith

# Legacies of Faith

## The Catholic Churches of Stearns County

John Roscoe
Robert Roscoe

Photographs by
Doug Ohman

North Star Press of St. Cloud, Inc.

Printed in the United States of America

ISBN10: 0-87839-314-5
ISBN13: 978-0-87839-314-5

Published by
North Star Press of St. Cloud, Inc
PO Box 451
St. Cloud, MN 56302

# Table of Contents

Preface . . . . . . . . . . . . . . . . . . . . . . . . . . . . . . . . . . . . . . . . . . . . . . vii
Introduction . . . . . . . . . . . . . . . . . . . . . . . . . . . . . . . . . . . . . . . . . . 1
Settlement History of Stearns County . . . . . . . . . . . . . . . . . . . . 4
Architecture of the Churches . . . . . . . . . . . . . . . . . . . . . . . . . . 12

**Part One: Early Churches** . . . . . . . . . . . . . . . . . . . . . . . . . . . . 27
Albany, Church of the Seven Dolors . . . . . . . . . . . . . . . . . . . . . 29
Avon, Church of St. Benedict . . . . . . . . . . . . . . . . . . . . . . . . . . 35
Collegeville, Parish of St. John the Baptist . . . . . . . . . . . . . . . . 39
Eden Valley, Church of the Assumption . . . . . . . . . . . . . . . . . . 41
Elrosa, Church of Sts. Peter and Paul . . . . . . . . . . . . . . . . . . . 45
Farming, Church of St. Catherine . . . . . . . . . . . . . . . . . . . . . . 51
Freeport, Church of the Sacred Heart . . . . . . . . . . . . . . . . . . . 55
Holdingford, Church of St. Mary . . . . . . . . . . . . . . . . . . . . . . . 61
Holdingford, Church of St. Hedwig . . . . . . . . . . . . . . . . . . . . . 63
Jacob's Prairie, Church of St. James . . . . . . . . . . . . . . . . . . . . 67
Lake Henry, Church of St. Margaret . . . . . . . . . . . . . . . . . . . . 69
Luxemburg, Church of St. Wendelin . . . . . . . . . . . . . . . . . . . . 73
Marty, Church of the Holy Cross . . . . . . . . . . . . . . . . . . . . . . . 77
Meire Grove, Church of St. John . . . . . . . . . . . . . . . . . . . . . . . 81
Melrose, Church of St. Boniface . . . . . . . . . . . . . . . . . . . . . . . 85
New Munich, Church of the Immaculate Conception . . . . . . . . . . 89
Opole, Church of Mary of Mount Carmel . . . . . . . . . . . . . . . . . 93
Richmond, Church of Sts. Peter and Paul . . . . . . . . . . . . . . . . . 97
Rockville, Church of St. Mary of the Immaculate Conception . . . . . . . . 101
Roscoe, Church of St. Agnes . . . . . . . . . . . . . . . . . . . . . . . . . . 105
St. Anna, Church of the Immaculate Conception . . . . . . . . . . . . . . . 109
St. Anthony, Church of St. Anthony . . . . . . . . . . . . . . . . . . . . . 113
St. Augusta, Church of St. Mary Help of Christians . . . . . . . . . . . . . 115
St. Augusta, St. Boniface Chapel . . . . . . . . . . . . . . . . . . . . . . . 119
St. Cloud, Church of St. John Cantius . . . . . . . . . . . . . . . . . . . 121
St. Cloud, St. Mary's Cathedral . . . . . . . . . . . . . . . . . . . . . . . 123
St. Joseph, Church of St. Joseph . . . . . . . . . . . . . . . . . . . . . . . 129

St. Joseph, Sacred Heart Chapel . . . . . . . . . . . . . . . . . . . . . . . 133
St. Nicholas, Church of St. Nicholas . . . . . . . . . . . . . . . . . . . . . 137
St. Rosa, Church of St. Rose of Lima . . . . . . . . . . . . . . . . . . . . 141
St. Stephen, Church of St. Stephen . . . . . . . . . . . . . . . . . . . . . . 143
St. Wendel, Church of St. Columbkille . . . . . . . . . . . . . . . . . . . 147
Sauk Centre, Church of Our Lady of the Angels . . . . . . . . . . . . . . . 151
Sauk Centre, Church of St. Paul . . . . . . . . . . . . . . . . . . . . . . . 155
Spring Hill, Church of St. Michael . . . . . . . . . . . . . . . . . . . . . . 159
Waite Park, Church of St. Joseph . . . . . . . . . . . . . . . . . . . . . . 167

**Part Two: Modern Churches** . . . . . . . . . . . . . . . . . . . . . . . 171
Belgrade, Church of St. Francis de Sales . . . . . . . . . . . . . . . . . . . 173
Brooten, Church of St. Donatus . . . . . . . . . . . . . . . . . . . . . . . 177
Cold Spring, Assumption Chapel . . . . . . . . . . . . . . . . . . . . . . . 179
Cold Spring, Church of St. Boniface . . . . . . . . . . . . . . . . . . . . . 181
Collegeville, St. John's Abbey . . . . . . . . . . . . . . . . . . . . . . . . 183
Greenwald, Church of St. Andrew . . . . . . . . . . . . . . . . . . . . . . 187
Kimball, Church of St. Anne . . . . . . . . . . . . . . . . . . . . . . . . . 191
Paynesville, Church of St. Louis . . . . . . . . . . . . . . . . . . . . . . . 195
St. Cloud, Christ Church . . . . . . . . . . . . . . . . . . . . . . . . . . . 197
St. Cloud, Church of St. Anthony . . . . . . . . . . . . . . . . . . . . . . 201
St. Cloud Church of the Holy Spirit . . . . . . . . . . . . . . . . . . . . . 203
St. Cloud, Church of St. Michael . . . . . . . . . . . . . . . . . . . . . . . 207
St. Cloud, Church of St. Paul . . . . . . . . . . . . . . . . . . . . . . . . 209
St. Cloud, Church of St. Peter . . . . . . . . . . . . . . . . . . . . . . . . 211
St. Francis, Church of St. Francis . . . . . . . . . . . . . . . . . . . . . . 213
St. Martin, Church of St. Martin . . . . . . . . . . . . . . . . . . . . . . . 217
Sartell, Church of St. Francis Xavier . . . . . . . . . . . . . . . . . . . . . 221

Glossary . . . . . . . . . . . . . . . . . . . . . . . . . . . . . . . . . 225
Bibliography . . . . . . . . . . . . . . . . . . . . . . . . . . . . . . . . 229
Acknowledgements . . . . . . . . . . . . . . . . . . . . . . . . . . . . . 230
About the Authors . . . . . . . . . . . . . . . . . . . . . . . . . . . 231

# Preface

The reader may be inclined to ask what caused us to write this book. The fact that we grew up in a strong Catholic family in northern Minnesota would seem to suggest that as an influence, but probably not entirely. The answer more likely resides in history and architecture. John's educational career resonates with the land and culture of Stearns County, where he and his wife have lived all their adult lives. For Robert, the practice of architecture and a deep daily devotion to historic preservation has become an indelible imprint. In the writing of this book, these factors were integral working parts of our combined value system.

We would also be remiss if we didn't mention the "church tours" around Stearns County at which time the idea of writing the book was conceived. Our brother Bill had come to Minnesota for a family visit and suggested we take a drive to search for shops that sell folk art. We headed out into Stearns County, and before long, spotted a church steeple on the horizon. Bill never passes a church without stopping in to see it, and soon we had visited several. As we sat in a pew at the Church of Seven Dolors in Albany beholding the beauty and grandeur of its interior, a shock of realization hit us. The architecture we were seeing surpassed all but a few of the churches recently visited in rural northern Italy—carefully proportioned features, sensitively rendered detail, and overall magnificence. Continued trips in Stearns County further confirmed this realization and inspired us to commit our thoughts and observations to words.

So—indeed a spirit moves us. These masonry edifices mysteriously evoke within us an aesthetic feeling and religious attentiveness, ironically, both being intangible and imbedded with a quiet presence that invites and excites the soul.

That familiar saying, "One picture is worth a thousand words" may be understated in what our book portrays. Doug Ohman, well known as a photographer of Minnesota places of history, gives us so many superlative images of the salutary attributes each church offers us. Doug has guided our minds and our footsteps which have amplified our understanding of these religious structures.

The German romantic era writer Johann Wolfgang Goethe stated, "Architecture is frozen music." If his words seem most applicable to places of worship, we can thank Doug Ohman's photography for capturing and holding the architecture of these magnificent churches of Stearns County.

# INTRODUCTION
# Legacies of Faith

Places of worship are guides in the landscape for local people who pass by them during their day-to-day routines. Even for members of the public at large, their physical familiarity affirms a sense of belonging to an environment that provides the sense of stability many of us seek. Upon entering these churches, the bright expanse of daylight becomes shrouded by the dark confines of the vestibule; then passing into the nave, one beholds a rich array of shadows and light among intricate, molded plaster features and expansive ceiling forms, while brilliant stained glass windows translate sunlight into intense colors. The experience can be transformative.

One of Winston Churchill's well-known quotations states: "We create buildings, and they create us." In another sense, local parishioners create places of worship, and these places, over time, create parishes as the heritage of a particular locality, measured by faith, tradition, and community spirit. In turn, these buildings foster pride, devotion, and generational cohesiveness in the community. Perhaps nowhere is this symbiosis more evident than in Stearns County, Minnesota.

This west-central section of Minnesota contains a generous sprinkling of small communities with handsome Catholic churches. Most of these towns were formed as, and still are, predominately Catholic settlements. No county in Minnesota, or even in the United States, compares in density of Catholic hamlets to Stearns County. With a population approximately sixty-six percent Catholic, this county contains fifty-two Catholic churches, the majority of which were built between 1871 and 1931. These edifices are remarkably similar in architectural style and quality to Catholic churches built in the hamlets of Germany where Stearns County's first European

emigrants originated. What is remarkable is that all but a few of the them are in excellent condition, typically are unaltered from their original construction and are continuing their original function as places of worship.

Polish settlers arrived in the United States in the 1870s and 1880s, their purpose being to live their Catholic faith and culture. Poland had been taken over by Germany, Russia, and Austria. In America, they clustered together to keep their language and culture alive. In Stearns County, desiring to establish their own identity, these immigrants organized their own parishes and found Polish priests. But they also sought to assimilate into the dominant German culture and chose to build their churches in the prevailing German style. Polish and other East European immigrant groups founded settlements that were relatively small, as were the churches they built. In neighboring counties where Polish settlement was much larger, the churches were larger, and the architecture more reflective of their homeland.

This high percentage of Catholic residents has created a cohesive culture, signified by the remarkable architecture of their churches. These structures came into being from extraordinary circumstances, which this book will delineate through historical, social and ethnic analysis, as well as by architectural research. The churches deserve greater awareness and attention for their architectural excellence, which contributes so strongly to the history of Minnesota and have endowed the state with a strong and well-defined regional force, thus far, greatly under-appreciated. These churches, most often being the largest and most architecturally imposing structures for miles around, seem somehow hidden in the wide open spaces of Minnesota prairie.

In the central core of Stearns County, the churches are clustered close to each other, sometimes no more than five miles apart. This culturally distinct aspect has few parallels in the nation. In the relatively flat farmland terrain, they become iconic structures, their slender spires seen from many miles away. As one approaches them, it becomes evident they serve as the center of the town or hamlet built around them and patterned after their Northern European counterparts.

Strongly German inspired, all but one of the churches are brick or stone. This German presence predominates most of Stearns County Catholic churches, even though Irish and Slovenian immigrants, in smaller numbers, also settled the area, and several Polish hamlets were established a generation after initial German settlement. Their masonry walls, made of stone and brick in stout thickness, serve three purposes: the high walls provide support for expansive spans of ceiling structure, are impervious to the rigors of Minnesota weather and require minimal maintenance. The physical permanence of these structures augments the strongly tradition-based life and culture of area residents.

## CULTURAL AND ARCHITECTURAL IMPORTANCE

The role of churches as centers of faith in communities is well known. But the power of their presence as community symbols invites more elucidation. Religious structures are the one unchanging element that buttresses against change and establishes forbearance against destruction, observes Alan Lathrop, author of the book *Churches of Minnesota*. This factor, over time, has reinforced the human desire to create churches crafted in rich detail.

This penchant for permanence arises out of the transitory aspects of life in agricultural communities, where the vagaries of weather on the farmers' crops and the effects of markets on storekeepers' ledgers can drastically influence the lives and well-being of families and communities. With these continual uncertainties, church structures offer the familiar, the enduring. Their immutable substantiality, symbolizing faith and life, have become a physical aspect of permanence. Some may ask why Catholic churches are built with brick while many Protestant churches are built with wood framing and siding. The answer may lie in the fundamental nature of the two beliefs. Catholic parishes tend to invest in the wealth of materiality to show the primacy of God over human lives, whereas Protestant congregations emphasize man's individual relationship to God as primary, conversely becoming expressed by less emphasis on overt materiality. A more basic reason may be with German traditional building methods that favor brick. Some architectural historians note that it is possible to chart German settlement areas in the Midwest by the frequent appearance of brick.

Churches are unlike other architectural building types that come and go. Traditional school buildings have become flattened into one story structures, and once stately Victorian houses have been replaced with more anonymous stripped-down forms. Even more drastic, railroad stations have disappeared altogether, and cooperative grain elevators that once competed with churches as local iconic landmarks are disappearing from the landscapes.

Seven of the churches in Stearns County are listed in the National Register of Historic Places. They meet the eligibility requirements of architectural distinctiveness, social relevance, and a formative role in community life.

In summary, the strong architectural significance of these Stearns County Catholic churches is their peerless quality of ecclesiastical architecture. This is what *Legacies of Faith* intends to communicate. These cultural icons can be architecturally infused cultural lessons for citizens of Minnesota and beyond.

# Settlement History of Stearns County

The presence of these impressive churches in Stearns County has its origins in the early 1850s shortly after the Minnesota Territory had been established in 1849. Before that time, most of what is now central and northern Minnesota had been inhabited by Native Americans. The Ojibway had moved westward from the Great Lakes region and eventually down to the central part of the state. The Dakota occupied the lands to the south and west. The dividing line between the two tribes actually ran across Stearns County.

Beginning in the seventeenth century, much of the western lands, including the area that is now Minnesota, came under the political control of France and later Great Britain and Spain. The French had three objectives for their new territory: to explore and map the region, to engage in the lucrative business of fur trading, and to convert the natives to Christianity. France ruled the area until the Spain took control of the areas west of the Mississippi in 1762, and Great Britain claimed the territory east of the river in 1763. Under both Great Britain and Spain, the exploration and fur trading continued.

As a result of the Louisiana Purchase of 1803, the western lands came under control of the United States, but heavy settlement by whites did not begin until treaties had been negotiated with the tribes living in the region. An 1837 treaty with the Ojibway opened the area between the Mississippi River and the St. Croix River to settlement. For many years Sauk Rapids, lying across the river from St. Cloud was the last settlement for whites on the frontier. In the Traverse d' Sioux Treaty of 1851, large tracts of land west of the Mississippi were opened. This event signaled the rapid growth that was to take place in Stearns County over the next fifty years. The fact that the great majority of the settlers were German Catholics can probably be attributed to the efforts of a Slovenian born missionary priest, Father Francis X. Pierz.

## FATHER FRANCIS XAVIER PIERZ

Father Pierz was born in what is now Slovenia in the old Austro-Hungarian empire in 1785. As a young man he studied for the priesthood and was ordained in Ljubljana in 1813. For the next twenty-two years, he served as a parish priest in his homeland. In 1835 Father Pierz answered the call to become a missionary to the Native Americans in the Great Lakes region. He arrived in America in the same year and spent the next seventeen years among the tribes in Michigan.

Meanwhile, in 1850, one year after the Minnesota Territory was established, the Diocese of St. Paul was formed, and Joseph Cretin was appointed Bishop. The new diocese was large, including the entire territory of Minnesota. Bishop Cretin was in dire need of priests to serve the increasing numbers of people coming into the region. He contacted the Diocese of Detroit and requested the services of Father Pierz, whose abilities as a missionary were well known. Pierz arrived in St. Paul in 1852 at the age of sixty-seven. Bishop Cretin put him in charge of the Indians and whites in the area along the Mississippi north to Crow Wing near the present city of Brainerd. Within his first year, Father Pierz had built a church at Crow Wing, and in 1853 he had built churches at nearby Belle Prairie and at Sauk Rapids, just across the river from St. Cloud.

With the opening of the lands west of the river to settlement in 1851, Father Pierz realized that the territory would be soon settled solely by white men. He also knew that the Sauk River Valley, which ran through the present Stearns County contained an abundance of fertile land very suitable for farming. There would also be opportunities for those who would want to start businesses on the new frontier. A self-taught agronomist, Father Pierz envisioned this area as a very desirable place for emigrants from his own European homeland to settle. He wrote several articles and advertisements in German Catholic publications in the eastern United States and Central Europe about the opportunities for farmers, merchants, and trades people to settle in this area. In an article in *Wahrheitsfreund*, a German Catholic newspaper published in Cincinnati in March of 1854 he wrote, "I do wish, however that the choicest pieces of land in this delightful Territory would become the property of thrifty Catholics who would make an earthly paradise of this Minnesota, which heaven has so richly blessed, and who would bear out the opinion that Germans prove to be the best farmers and the best Christians in America. I am sure that you will likewise do credit to your faith here in Minnesota, but to prove yourselves good Catholics do not bring with you any freethinkers, red republicans, atheists or agitators."

Father Pierz. (Photo courtesy Stearns History Museum)

The response was enthusiastic, and the first settlers arrived in 1855. Many came from parts of the United States where Germans had settled earlier. Large numbers came from Ohio, Maryland, Wisconsin, Missouri, and Indiana. Based on writings in publications in Germany and Austria, other settlers came to Minnesota directly from Europe. By 1860, the population of Stearns County had reached over 4,000 settlers, almost all of them German Catholics, and by 1870 the population had reached 14,000. According to an 1880 census, it had risen to 22,000. By the time the heavy immigration had abated in 1900, the population of Stearns County was 44,000. Other census data indicated that within certain townships in Stearns County, seventy-five percent or more of the households were headed by Germans.

Father Pierz remained in Stearns County and the immediate area to the north and west of Stearns for two years, from 1854 until 1856, and for most of this time traveled on foot throughout the county offering mass and sacraments in the rapidly growing German settlements. Nearing seventy years old, Pierz was slight of build and his back was stooped from carrying a sack with articles for saying mass from settlement to settlement. His first mission in Stearns County was in St. Cloud where he bought land and built a modest frame church. During the next two years he was responsible for the formation of several other parishes including St. Augusta, St. Joseph, Jacobs Prairie, and Richmond. He also visited settlements as far west as Spring Hill and Lake Henry. Father Pierz soon realized that he would need many more priests to serve these settlements, and he called upon Bishop Cretin for help. Cretin contacted St. Vincent's, a Benedictine Monastery in Latrobe, Pennsylvania, and they agreed to send priests. The first group arrived in St. Cloud in 1856 and took up the task of serving the numerous German settlements. Meanwhile, Father Pierz returned to his missionary work among the Indians further north. In his earlier search for more priests, he had made appeals to his homeland, but to no avail. On a visit back to Slovenia during the winter of 1863-1864 he was more successful. Sixteen young men, one of them a priest and the others seminarians, agreed to come to America and join him in his missionary work. One of the seminarians, James Trobec, later became the third bishop of the Diocese of St. Cloud.

After nearly twenty years as a missionary in Minnesota, Father Pierz retired and moved to Rich Prairie (now Pierz) in Morrison County as pastor. Two years later in 1873, he returned to his native Slovenia where he died on January 22, 1880 at the age of ninety-five.

## THE BENEDICTINES AND THE GROWTH OF PARISHES

The first Benedictine priests from Pennsylvania arrived in St. Cloud on May 20, 1856, and made their way to the chapel, which Father Pierz had built earlier in nearby Sauk Rapids. There Father Pierz had left items necessary for saying mass, including vestments for the priests. He also left instructions with the locations of the settlements he had visited previously. The priests wasted little time in beginning their work. The day after their arrival, mass was held in St. Cloud. Then they spread out to the other settlements, saying mass and administering sacraments. The people were happy to see them and even happier that they spoke German. Despite the arrival of the first three priests in 1856, masses were still irregular in most of the settlements, usually occurring once per month.

One of the first tasks for the Benedictines was to formally organize parishes into a cohesive unit. Although there was no lack of faith among the settlers, the fact that they had come from a number of areas in the east and were consumed with the task of building shelters and opening the land made it necessary that they be brought together as a faith community. To accomplish this, the Benedictines brought in a well-known Jesuit priest, Father Francis Weninger to conduct missions in the new settlements. The missions consisted of four sermons a day in addition to other prayers and devotions. At each site a mission cross was erected, several of which have survived to this day, including those in St. Augusta and Farming.

After a number of years in St. Cloud, the Benedictines purchased land west of St. Joseph and built a monastery there originally called St. Louis on the Lake, later becoming St. John's Abbey and University. The seminary trained a great number of priests, who would later serve parishes throughout Stearns County and beyond. The Richmond and St. Joseph parishes served as mission centers for the rest of the county where Benedictine priests were sent out to the settlements further west. Like Father Pierz, these priests walked to the new settlements carrying a sack over their back that contained all the items needed to say mass. One of these priests, Father Clement Staub, is credited with saying the first mass and organizing five parishes in western Stearns County including New Munich, Meire Grove, St. Martin, Lake Henry, and Lake George (Elrosa). During the years from 1856 to the mid-1880s the Benedictines were responsible for the formation of twenty-five additional parishes to the five that Father Pierz had founded earlier.

## THE BENEDICTINES LOSE THEIR PARISHES

During the period from the early 1850s until 1875, all the parishes in Stearns County were part of the Diocese of St. Paul. In 1875, due to the rapid settlement of the areas north of St. Paul, Bishop Cretin established the Vicariate of Northern Minnesota, and installed Abbot Rupert Seidenbusch of St. John's Abbey as Vicar Apostolic. The vicariate was simply a subdivision of the larger Diocese of St. Paul. Abbot Seidenbusch presided over the parishes and missions in central and northern Minnesota. This structure remained until 1889 when a separate Diocese of St. Cloud was established. In order that the new diocese in St. Cloud wasn't to be considered an extension of the Benedictine Order, the Archbishop dissolved the vicariate, and Otto Zardetti became the bishop of the new diocese. The Benedictines were given charge of ten parishes in perpetuity, Pastors for the rest of the parishes were secular priests, meaning they had no affiliation with any religious order.

## OTHER ETHNIC IMMIGRATION PATTERNS

The influx of Germans into Stearns County came not only from other states where they had previously settled, but from their homeland as well, and they tended to settle in areas according to their region of origin. The area around Cold Spring was largely Bavarian, while those in St. Augusta were Westphalians, and around Luxemburg were Luxembourgers. Also during this period several other ethnic groups arrived.

## IRISH

Irish immigrants came to the United States as a result of political oppression and the ensuing poverty caused by the potato crop failures. As with the other immigrant groups coming to Stearns County in the latter half of the nineteenth century, Catholicism was an important part of their ethnicity. Most settled in the eastern part of the country. In Minnesota, some of the early Irish established farms in southeastern part of the state and as railroad workers in the Twin Cities. In Stearns County many Irish also worked for the newly expanding railroad in St. Cloud, Melrose, and Sauk Centre. Another group settled the St. Wendel area as farmers. In the early parts of the immigration the churches that the Irish formed were the only English-speaking Catholic churches in Stearns County. In Melrose the first Catholic parish, St. Patrick's, had been established well before heavy German settlement had begun. The result was that, for many years, there were two Catholic churches in Melrose, one Irish and the other German. In nearby Sauk Centre, Irish immigrants broke away from the predominately German St. Paul's parish and established Our Lady of the Angels Church. Over the years the number of Irish declined in the area, many moving to the Minneapolis and St. Paul to work with the railroad and other businesses.

## POLISH AND SLOVENIAN SETTLEMENT

Emigrants from Poland arrived in central Minnesota nearly twenty years after the Germans and organized parishes in the northeastern part of Stearns County in the towns of Opole and Holdingford, and also in St Cloud and St. Anna. Most of the Poles were farmers and came to America to escape religious and economic oppression in their homeland, which had been taken over by its geographic neighbors, Prussia, Austria, and Russia. The majority of the Polish came from the province of Silesia, and had an intense desire to preserve their own culture, later starting their own parishes where they could hear the sermons in their own language. The bishops were sympathetic to their plight and made sure that Polish-speaking priests were made available to them. In Holdingford and St. Cloud the Polish churches were built in towns where a German church already existed. These parishes were called national parishes

meaning that the reason for their existence was to serve people of one nationality. Today, that designation no longer applies, and Catholics of any nationality may attend them.

When Father Pierz returned to his native Slovenia for a visit in 1864, he convinced a number of his countrymen to settle in Minnesota. He originally had some land in mind in the Ottertail area, but he later learned that the land had been taken by others. The Slovenians eventually settled in the northeast corner of Stearns County in Brockway Township and founded the town of St. Stephen, the first Slovenian settlement in the United States. Others pushed further west in the county around the present town of St. Anthony.

## THE GROWTH OF TOWNS

Within the first three decades following the initial settlement of Stearns County in 1854-1855, the population grew at a rapid rate, influencing the growth of towns. Although the earliest settlements were in St. Cloud and the immediate vicinity, by 1857 there were settlements as far away as the Elrosa area, about forty miles away near the western border of Stearns County. In most cases, the settlers followed the path of the oxcart trails along the Sauk River, which had been established earlier to move furs from far northwestern Minnesota to St. Paul. Another trail, which ran northwest from St. Cloud roughly along the path of the present interstate highway, provided access to the central and northwestern parts of the county. The transition from settlement clusters to towns occurred gradually, and was influenced by two main factors: church locations and the coming of railroads.

## THE INFLUENCE OF CHURCHES

Soon after a number of settlers had arrived in a particular area, they petitioned for a priest to visit them and say mass and perform sacraments. The first services were held in homes, but soon after a modest church was built, usually a log structure. As the population of the area grew, a larger church was constructed, and often a small hamlet grew up around it. This church was usually at a central location within the settlement and at the intersection of the main roads. It usually consisted of the church, a school, and a few small farm-related businesses such as a blacksmith shop and a creamery. Some hamlets eventually got a post office as well. Later a few houses were also constructed. Over time the church became not only the spiritual center of the community but the social and cultural center as well. The influence of the church in these small communities is reflected in the fact that eleven of them in Stearns County have saint's names.

In some cases the churches were built before the town where they were located was platted, and in many cases the town was never platted. For a long time these towns were relatively self-sufficient in that there were businesses there to meet the majority of the services needed. Eventually, due to better roads and more centralization of businesses, many of the original businesses in the towns closed.

Larger towns throughout the county became the main service centers. Today, driving through the rural parts of Stearns County one can find many small villages that are largely unchanged from the earlier settlement days. There may be a number of homes, a bar, and a gas station, but it would be obvious that the Catholic church in those towns is still the center of community life.

## INFLUENCE OF RAILROADS

Another pivotal factor in the growth of towns came with the expansion of railroads through Stearns County. Beginning in the early 1870s, the St Paul Minneapolis and Manitoba Railroad laid tracks from St. Cloud westerly through Stearns County to Sauk Centre. In many cases Yankee speculators bought up land along the path of the railroad where stations were to be built, and the ensuing growth made these towns trade centers for a wide area around them. Examples of such railroad towns are Albany, Melrose, and Sauk Centre.

In the early part of the twentieth century, the Soo Line was built through the county in a north to south direction. Again, where the railroad established stations, towns grew, while towns bypassed by the railroad often died. This happened in western Stearns County where the railroad was responsible for the growth of Elrosa, while the nearby settlement of Lake George died. As a whole, the railroads were very instrumental not only in the growth of towns but in the expansion of the agricultural base by providing a means for farm products to be marketed.

## STEARNS COUNTY TODAY

From a population of nearly 50,000 in 1900, the county has grown to 133,000 in 2000 according to Census Bureau figures. Nearly three-fourths of the inhabitants live in the St. Cloud area on the eastern edge of the county. From early on, St. Cloud has been the county seat as well as the commercial hub for the central Minnesota area, and the population there continues to grow. The rural area has seen a slight dip in population but remains predominately agricultural with small and medium-size dairy farms as the mainstay of the economy. It should be noted that many of the farms have stayed in the families of their original owners to this day. As of the year 2000, there were 334 Century Farms listed by the Stearns County History Museum, nearly one-third of all dairy farms in the county. Century Farm designation means the farm has stayed in the hands of the same family for at least 100 years. It is also of interest to note that in the year 2000, approximately sixty percent of all inhabitants of Stearns County claimed Germany as their country of origin.

Catholicity remains strong in Stearns County as well. According to the Association of Religion Data Archives, sixty-two percent of all persons claiming religious affiliation in Stearns County are Catholic. That percentage is undoubtedly much higher in the rural part of the county. The number of Catholic parishes in the county also remains very stable. From forty-five parishes in 1916, the number is now forty-nine. Eight new parishes were formed from the years of 1926 to 1972, while four parishes closed. The new parishes are mostly in St. Cloud and were formed as a result of population growth, while the closures occurred mostly in the rural part of the county due to a decline in numbers and mergers with other parishes. One of the churches, Sacred Heart in Arban near St. Anna, had been listed on the National Register of Historic Places. It was moved to Albany where it became part of the Pioneer Park there.

In the early years of the initial settlement, one priest often served the spiritual needs of several parishes. Ironically, in the present, due to a shortage of clergy, this has again become the norm. Only a few of the largest of the parishes have their own priest. In the majority of cases, one priest serves two or more congregations.

# The Architecture
of the Churches

Many of the Catholic churches in Stearns County bear a substantial resemblance to Catholic churches in the regions of Germany where many first-generation Stearns County residents came from. The Church of Saint John the Baptist in Meire Grove built in 1885 (prior to its 1923 successor), according to architectural historian Fred W. Peterson, is based on Gothic-Romanesque parish churches of northwestern Germany, such as the Church of Saints Peter and Paul in Holdorf. This example appears in many hamlets throughout the area. Often the large brick church, accompanied by the rectory that houses the clergy, is surrounded on the main street by general merchandise stores, farm implement dealers, a blacksmith shop, and a one or two saloons, marking the center of the community.

Similarly, there are a few churches in Polish communities and other Eastern European emigrant hamlets that represent certain aspects of the towns of Eastern Europe, although, for the most part, the basic architecture of Eastern European-influenced edifices follow the German model. These European immigrants brought to Stearns County whatever household items they could carry, but they also brought many values and customs from their Old World culture, where tradition guided so much of their ancestors' lives. The large number of German-based communities, strengthened by a tradition of organization and unified by faith and ethnic background, became a dominant cultural force. According to Peterson, in his book *Building Community—Keeping the Faith*, a significant result was German parishioners "remained insulated from many of the pressures of the dominant Anglo-American culture." This reinforced their propensity to build their churches with a common vocabulary of architectural design.

Although many brick houses throughout the hamlets and farmsteads of Stearns County are based on houses in Germany, they exhibit adaptations for local conditions that vary from the Old Country. The German churches however, as well as several Polish edifices, are more direct translations from the Old Country. So the question is: why was this architectural fidelity necessary? Architectural historian Robert Ferguson formulated this answer: These conservative, practical-minded Germans and East Europeans lived by traditional methods, whether for farming practices or raising children. Pragmatic farm buildings could be adapted casually, but the church played a role in the community that was more analogous to raising children: it provided a kind of education. Far more than farms or even houses, the church had to represent the community, both to outsiders and to the community itself. And with nineteenth-century attitudes toward architectural style as representative of ethnic identity, stylistic awareness, if not always literal correctness, was vital.

## BUILDING THE CHURCHES

Parish by parish, Stearns County community church building followed a pattern of modest original structures and construction to meet parish growth, and also as a response to occasional destruction by fire. Typically, a makeshift log building served as their first church. Somewhat later, their first "established" church was wood-frame, built almost entirely by local labor with framing lumber produced by nearby sawmills and other building materials transported from the nearby railroad depots. In effect, this second effort served as a "starter" church, training the parishioners in fundraising, the physical organizing needed to mobilize construction, and the deepening and building of faith to inspire building. When the parish expanded beyond the size of their wood frame church, they had the capacity and devotion to build the much larger masonry-structured church.

When it came time to construct the brick places of worship, design of these larger churches required more structural expertise, which in turn required more professional construction methods. Architects stepped into the role of church design, selected through diocese recommendations or by a priest with prior experience in church construction. The architects came from a few firms in St. Cloud, several in Minneapolis and Saint Paul, and a number in Wisconsin. German names invariably appeared in the architectural firm names. The Wisconsin architectural firm Parkinson and Dockendorff was headed by German immigrants. The much larger and more complicated work of these churches typically required a building contractor, instead of a coterie of local craftsmen such as those who built the wood-framed churches. These contractors were selected based on their experience in the area and their ability to undertake this scale of endeavor. In some instances, however, local volunteer labor was used for some work, such as hauling granite foundation material used for construction.

## ARCHITECTURAL COMPONENTS OF THE CHURCHES

The traditional Catholic church floor plan changed very little from the early Christian fourth-century A.D. era to the early decades of the twentieth century. The primary spatial components are the nave, a main space which encompasses the seating; the sanctuary, where the priest and attendants perform the religious services; and the narthex, the chamber serving as the entrance. Typically, the floor plan of these churches formed the shape of a cross, with the long lower shaft being the narthex and the nave, the arms extending outward, forming the transept, and the cross's top serving as the sanctuary.

Liturgically, the altar is the most important element of the church interior, and the whole sanctuary is designed to focus the eyes of the faithful on the altar, amplifying the importance of the religious event. This significance becomes heightened, literally, by the elevation of the sanctuary floor a few steps above the floor of the nave. The back of the altar is set against or partially under elaborately and conspicuously assembled ornamental structures. The earlier more Gothic-inspired churches used intricate and vertically-ordered mini-spired assemblages called reredos, and the more Romanesque-influenced later churches formed baldachin canopies, usually supported by columns, all rendered with overt embellishment. The space terminating the sanctuary is the apse, often half-round or half-octagonal in shape, covered by a segmented dome-shaped roof.

## FLOOR PLAN

Smaller churches have side walls built straight upward, which typically support a vaulted clear-span roof, all of which encompass the nave. Larger churches employ a basilica plan with origins in pre-Christian buildings that evolved over two millennia. The basilica plan is based on the nave between two side aisles. The nave is a central space of considerable height, whose upper walls are supported by series of substantial columns flanked by relatively narrow side aisles. The columns' structural function is evident enough, but less obvious is their role of leading the eye upward to the higher glory of the architectural spaces of the ceiling. The spaces between the columns are often arched, which serves structurally to transfer wall and roof loads to the series of columns, as well as presenting a local rhythm lending cadence to the length of the nave. Also, these arched openings provide spatial access to the side aisles that are often covered by lower roofs, unifying many rows of pews within the total nave envelope. The section of the upper wall of the nave rising above the aisle roofs is called the clerestory, which usually contains regularly spaced tall stained glass windows, which provide intricately patterned multi-color light and lend a lofty character to the nave's upper reaches. The choir loft, a balcony built over the inner narthex doors that gives an entrance to the nave, serves to sequence the entrant's expanding visual experience. With the choir situated above and behind the people, voices raised in song float over the congregants, while their eyes are fixed forward on the visually evocative, symbolic features, all to suggest to the senses a hint of the everlasting to come.

The third spatial component, the narthex, serves as an entrance space, managing the transition from exterior to interior. The relatively low ceiling, which supports the choir loft above, leads churchgoers into a symbolic interval, separating the ecclesiastical prominence of the facade in relation to the sky, preparing the entrant for the solemnity and visual grandeur of the interior.

## SPACE

It should be noted that architecture is not only made up of the visible surfaces of walls, floors, roofs, and ceilings; those elements are the containers that hold, shape and define a building's most important attribute–space–which defines the purpose for the structure's being. Obviously, space itself cannot be viewed as such, but we know it by its form, molded by its defining surfaces. As architect-philosophers Charles Moore and Donlyn Lyndon note in their book, *Chambers for a Memory Palace*, space is not empty nothingness, but "more like what the Chinese call chi, which means something between space and spirit." Perhaps there is no more eloquent experience of chi-infused space than Gothic cathedrals, where the vertical stretches of vaulted space stir our feelings, and we achieve awareness of space as an attribute

co-equal to the physicality of enclosure. The principal attribute of Gothic cathedrals, the churches of European countrysides, and places of worship in Stearns County is the fusing of what the eyes see and what is revealed to the soul. Gothic master builders developed an aesthetic in which the experience unfolds in sequence (which likewise is necessarily true in music and dance because of their reliance on time). The most successful visual arts allow the eye to linger and extend a retinal reaction into an aesthetic moment. With Gothic cathedrals, the architecture presents us with staged sequences that lead the eyes at various paces, interweaving space and form as our eyes follow, glimpsing detail in measured intervals.

## ORNAMENT

Ornament does not serve as merely embellishment in itself in the most noble works of architecture. In architectural terms, ornament of wall spaces creates a hierarchical system serving as a control mechanism to create visual order for the complexity of interior structure. Ornament's companion purpose is likewise functional, serving religious purposes of symbolic references. In Gothic

churches, and the Gothic-Romanesque churches in Stearns County, detail features are often rendered in a profusion that induces the mind to dissolve away its quotidian thoughts in order to concentrate on the matter at hand, which is worship. But the purpose of religion is to extend its guidance beyond the ceremony of worship and beyond the walls of the place of worship. The architectural experience serves to carry faith into daily life.

## ART: STATUARY, PAINTINGS, PIPE ORGANS

The function of art in the churches does not fall into the category of "art for art's sake." As with the architectural features, statues, wall paintings, crucifixes, stations of the cross, and pipe organs serve as reinforcement to form devotion, with their aesthetic qualities intended to enhance that role.

Church records carry little information as to their origins, but nineteenth-century church construction depended on furnishings of artwork, such as crucifixes and stations of the cross. This artwork is said to have come from religious art supply companies in the Twin Cities, Milwaukee, New York, and other American sources as well as Europe. Italian and German manufacturers exported religious art to this country.

Statues represent the holy family and various saints, and most often portray the saint for whom the church is named. These statues have significant prominence in Catholic churches, located immediately above the altar in elaborate ornamented niches within reredos and baldachins, and also in side altars where the statues become a major focus. In many instances, statues are incorporated into architecture rather than being set pieces to be observed separately.

Paintings are not as ubiquitous as statuary, and appear in only a few churches. The most notable use is in the ceiling at the Church of Saint Mary Help of Christians in Saint Augusta. These paintings appear to be on canvas, most likely imported, with artwork painted on the canvas at its site of origin and applied on site. The Church of the Sacred Heart at Freeport features an intricately detailed painting with mosaic-like background. At the Church of Saint Francis deSales in Belgrade, a large painting behind the altar called The Glorification of the Eucharist was painted in Rome and contributed by a parishioner. Large painted curved walled apse surfaces depict Christ images in several churches. The most striking one is at Saint John the Baptist in Meire Grove. A painted Christ child and Mary with a gold halo hovers over the altar at Saints Peter and Paul at Elrosa, and a recent example is the dramatic Assumption of Mary at the Church of Holy Angels in Sauk Centre, painted by a regional artist in 2004.

Pipe organs play a dual role in church aesthetics: rendering music as an integral part of services and as artwork in their own right.

## STAINED GLASS: ITS DEVELOPMENT, INFLUENCE ON GOTHIC ARCHITECTURE AND MEDIEVAL THEOLOGY

### ORIGINS

The origins of stained glass can be traced to the first century A.D., used domestically as luxury objects. The medium's original use in Christian churches began in the Constantinian era in the 4th century A.D., occasionally as an alternative to mosaics that served to provide panels of glittering surfaces to stone walls in Byzantine churches. By the 9th and 10th centuries, the Early Romanesque churches incorporated stained glass windows with linear patterns and frontal two-dimensional figures. The size of the windows were small in comparison those in the Gothic era, when advances in artisanship and technology made stained glass the monumental art form as we know it today. Stained glass windows contained old and new testament scenes that became visual lessons for the largely illiterate population. Some windows employed symbols as the subject matter, such as an eye in a triangular shape that represented the all-knowing and ever-present.

Visual literacy became an outcome of these stained glass works of art, just as cathedrals themselves became known as "the bible in stone." Artisan guilds donated windows that occasionally included likenesses of themselves at work with their craft. The main subject matter was often figures, with decorative borders using foliage and other naturalistic forms, as experimentation led to more formalized and intricate compositions.

## STAINED GLASS IN STEARNS COUNTY CATHOLIC CHURCHES

European cathedrals became the prototype for the much smaller sized churches throughout towns and villages in Germany and nearby provinces. Of course, county churches in nineteenth century America, much like their progenitors in Germany, are a different architectural type than Gothic cathedrals with their stone vaulting and greatly increased size. Nonetheless, the windows in cathedrals and country churches are similarly aligned in wall structure, and the application of stained glass is very similar.

First generation German immigrants in Stearns County were culture-bound to build new churches in strong likenesses to their homeland. Stained glass windows, which changed little in technology and subject matter from the Gothic era, could illuminate faith as they did for their medieval predecessors. This became more directly applied, as many Stearns churches installed stained glass windows fabricated in Europe.

Almost all of the early church windows have main sections with pointed or round arch tops, and much smaller lower sections having top-hinged panels that can swing inward for ventilation. A significant aspect of these windows is how the stained glass serves two purposes. The main panel gives religious instruction, and the lower hinged panels contain the name of the window's donor, serving to honor both the name of the benefactor and the ethnic identity–a small but important way that honors church history and family memory.

The exact sources of stained glass fabricators are largely unknown, not appearing in church records, but general knowledge indicates several companies in the twin cities and Milwaukee may have supplied many of the windows in this area. Gary Terhaar, owner of Terhaar Studios in Cold Spring, whose company has repaired numerous stained glass windows throughout Stearns County, commented that the type of high workmanship in these windows seem to indicate many windows may have come from Germany. Terhaar is a second generation stained glass window artist; his father learned the art and craft working on the fabrication of the large stained glass panels in the construction of Saint Johns Abbey Church in the late1950s.

Church by church, the stained glass in Stearns Catholic places of worship offer many forms of this art–in technique, subject matter, and stylistic change. Aesthetics may be the messenger, but subject matter is the message. Throughout the county, the lesson plan purpose of stained glass themes frequently portray enactments of the old testament and various gospels, figures

of saints who play significant roles in the faith, and an array of symbols representing basic faith attributes.

At the Church of Saint Catherine in Farming, the stained glass windows along the left side of the nave depict green robed female saints, and the right side features male saints, also in green robes. Green is one of several colors whose symbolic meaning derives from pre-Christian times, a pagan reference to initiation. In this case, the color denotes vegetation and spring, therefore the triumph of spring over winter. Other colors of garments have great symbolic meaning. Red can signify power, sometimes blood, and often martyrs wear red clothing. Blue is truth, as blue appears after clouds have passed, suggesting the unveiling of truth. Purple can refer to royalty and power, also sorrow and penitence. Purple also is typically used as preparation for Advent and Lent.

Today–stained glass in Stearns County worship places remains in operation, kept in good repair by parish budgetary balance sheets. Parishes scribe their business and events in records and notebooks, which eventually form parish history

Meanwhile, Sunday by Sunday, parish people gathering in the nave become illuminated by the shards of bright sunlit glass by the same sun that illuminated old instructions. And into their week, these people move their lives onward, to form shards of history. So the lessons of the stained glass continue–in faith- in history.

## SYMBOLIC FORMS

One noteworthy aspect of the overall design of the church building is to craft a structural symbol of the recurring numbers of two and three, with three being more prevalent. The ubiquitous role of the trinity is fundamental to Christian faith. Frequently found in the liturgy and rites of the faith, the number three is symbolized by the holy family, the pair of threes in Christ's age, the three wise men, and countless other examples. Architecturally, threes recur parts: the central high nave flanked by two lower aisles, the main altar and two side minor altars, and stained glass windows often have two arched panels bolstering a center round shape, or are fashioned so that the two arched panels set into the overall window frame that becomes the third panel.

Gothic churches, although having such strong masonry forms, hold an interior affinity for the mysterious. The lacy character of the nave ceiling vaults, according to many architectural historians, evokes a mystical affinity for forests as seen in ribbed edges for intersecting vaults, where the ribs simulate overhead criss-crossing branches. This observation is so poignantly echoed by Lyndon and Moore, who note that the churches of Germany, Poland and Czechoslovakia have "the most literally tree-like webs of ribbing . . . where all the piers are the same height, create uniform fields of space that are often built with vaults traced by networks of ribbing that spring without interruption from those piers, creating an arboreal cover for the congregation below."

## ARCHITECTURAL STYLES

The first churches built in Stearns County were Gothic in style, which was basically a structural-based building type for cathedrals in Western Europe and England built in the twelfth and thirteenth centuries A.D. The Gothic style is characterized by steep nave roofs, tall bell towers topped by slender spires and pointed arched windows, with interior intersecting vaulted ceilings. The Gothic of nineteenth-century Stearns County, however, differs from the Gothic Revival that had developed in England in the late eighteenth century and flourished on the American east coast by the 1840s. As historian Alan Gowans points out, the kind of Gothic that nineteenth-century Americans perceived as particularly German had a strong Romanesque flavor, as the Smithsonian "Castle" on the Washington, D.C., Mall, begun in 1849 by James Renwick, illustrates. In the Midwest, immigrants built churches with architectural features they remembered from their old world communities, and medieval German churches were as frequently Romanesque as Gothic, often mixing the two closely related vocabularies.

In nineteenth-century Germany, a Romanesque revival called the Rundbogenstil or round-arched style dominated monumental buildings from the 1820s through the 1840s, particularly in Bavaria. And a direct Minnesota connection was forged in 1870, when the largely Bavarian Assumption parish in Saint Paul began a towering new church designed by the Bavarian court architect Eduard Riedl. Translated into the rough local limestone, the elegant, Italianate Rundbogenstil took on a very different character.

The German-immigrant Minnesota and Wisconsin architects who designed for Stearns County, similarly, drew on a rich vocabulary of Gothic and Romanesque elements to produce churches that were neither doctrinaire Gothic nor Rundbogenstil, nor the "Richardsonian" Romanesque of the 1880s and 1890s, but that parishioners could identify with their memories of the Romanesque and Gothic in the old country. Sometimes an austere, red-brick exterior, with its Romanesque round arches and corbels, will give way to an ornate interior of Gothic verticality and light, rib vaults leading the eye and mind upward with that sense of reassurance that religious structures seek to express.

The demographics of the county provided another aspect of church architectural style evolution. In the 1880s, county settlement was primarily rural, mostly German, where the patterns of life were built on widely shared values, and the churches bear strong testimony to this characteristic. However, by the first decades of the twentieth century, rural growth had abated, while urban populations increased in numbers, along with ethnic and social diversity. Consequently, Catholic churches in larger towns and especially in St. Cloud took on more variable architectural expressions. Also, Catholic churches built after World War I seemed to depart from German-influenced design, but not, according to local historians, a consequence of anti-German reactions prevalent at that time.

## THE END OF THE GOTHIC/ROMANESQUE TRADITION

During the early twentieth century, Gothic-Romanesque architecture began to play itself out, in the way all styles end, whether in architecture, music, painting, dance or music. An undercurrent comes into being at some time during the reign of a prevailing style, at first coursing under the surface, then forcing occurrences out to play its tricks when the opportunity arises—invariably when the dominant style continues to repeat itself with caricatures of itself. In the case of central Minnesota Gothic-Romanesque ecclesiastical architecture, the late nineteenth century's cultural dependence on the Old World familiarity, that the Gothic-Romanesque dutifully delivered, became obsolete a few decades after the twentieth century arrived. America's sense of nationalism, bolstered by new technology able to offer comfort and convenience, ushered in a sense of confidence to imagine and embrace the new. When these changes arrived in the once-isolated rural areas, architecture began to seek new expression. As in all style shifts, the structural armature of Gothic-Romanesque provided a transition that appended oncoming forms of architectural expression.

From 1923 to 1931, the architects of several new Catholic churches looked back prior to the Gothic-Romanesque to the basilica form of the early Christian churches that featured straight-walled naves without transepts and flat exposed beam ceilings to their interiors. Traces of Byzantine architecture of the Eastern Roman Empire could be found in Romanesque Revival structures on the East Coast—and also in facets of Saint John the Baptist in Meire Grove and the Cathedral of Saint Mary in Saint Cloud. At the Church of the Holy Angels in Sauk Centre, the ambulatory in the apse is a direct recall of the early basilica plan. Eclectic architectural design motifs appeared in several places of worship: The church of Saint Andrew in Greenwald has Spanish-influenced elements appearing in Southwestern American churches, and Saint Agnes in Roscoe incorporates several Colonial Revival features in its façade.

The last churches built in Stearns County before World War II, were built in 1931, ending sixty years of early church construction in Stearns County.

## THE MODERN MOVEMENT BEGINS

The year 1954 signals the advent of modern architecture in Stearns County, with the construction of the Church of Saint Francis in the town of the same name. Four years later, Saint Peter's in Saint Cloud was built as an extended one-level structure incorporating a worship space with an elementary school, administrative offices, and a large commons area to serve various social and cultural activities that mid-twentieth-century life integrated into religious life. The church building no longer needed to serve as a stand-alone structure, when the basement was sufficient to accommodate church dinners, bingo, and other social activities, just as religion itself was no longer a stand-alone aspect of Catholic life. In these multi-use facilities, the worship structure was no longer a tall, dominating edifice, as religion's primacy changed into one component, although an over-arching one, to serve a more coordinating role. Physically as well as symbolically, the worship space roof became identifiable, though not often a significant form relating to the whole of the building complex.

During this time, long-standing parishes began to plan for expanded facilities, and new additions began to be built adjoining existing older churches. Generally, these new structures' use of brick continued and complemented existing churches, while their roof slopes departed from the steep pitches of the predominant structure. Exterior architectural features attempt to acknowledge the original church design while working with the vocabulary of contemporary architecture. Some new additions were built on the side of the original structure while others extended from the front façade. Interior spaces were designed for specific purposes while accommodating flexibility for many functions. Many of these additions provided handicap accessibility, including lift mechanisms for access to the main church floor, thereby extending elderly parishioners' years of worship.

There may be critics who find the contemporary design of these additions not to be in conformance with the traditional Gothic-Romanesque architecture of the original structures, believing the new addition should follow the original the style. However, a counter argument may be two-fold: the Gothic-Romanesque is vertically-oriented, by its purpose of elevating the sense of worship, but verticality in these addition situations is impractical. Moreover, history is the record of change, and new structures should architecturally express the spirit of the time in which they were built. By studying additions of places of worship in previous centuries, the distinction of styles becomes a facet of historical interest.

In 1961, the Abbey Church at Saint John's University in Collegeville, designed by Marcel Breuer, was built, and the contemporary cast-concrete structure quickly gained world-wide recognition as a significant example of twentieth-century architecture. In the following years, and up to the time of this writing, modern architecture has become the design archetype applied to nearly all Christian church construction.

## THE INFLUENCE OF VATICAN II

Vatican II was a process within the Catholic Church that sought reform in religious practices, to integrate modern human experience with Christian dogma. An important goal was to make the church "ecumenical," to build various types of relationships with other religious denominations. Beginning formal deliberations in 1961 and largely concluding four years later, its main effect on the Catholic population was the promulgation that the faithful should have active participation in liturgical celebrations. A practical outcome was reversing the altar to put the priest and attendants facing the parishioners allowing the congregation to receive communion by hand. Two consequential results were expansion of the altar platform slightly outside of the sanctuary and into the nave, and elimination of the communion railing where parishioners knelt on one side for the priest to administer the communion by mouth from the sanctuary side. Removal of the communion rail had a symbolic effect—putting priest and parishioners in a type of participatory communion.

It is very significant to note that two Stearns County Catholic edifices designed in the early 1960s anticipated Vatican II changes that modern design put into place—the Abbey Church at Saint John's University and Christ Church at the Newman Center at Saint Cloud State University. Shortly afterward, in all of the seven Catholic churches built subsequent to Vatican II's instructions, modern architecture's response provided fundamental change in Catholicism's practice of faith.

On one hand, these new churches provide for the fundamental aspects of religious worship. On the other hand, church design in the hands of modernist architects creates efficiency with spiritual context. Places of traditional worship with parishioners in a structured longitudinal nave that is relatively remote from the priest and attendants, who shape ritual services in highly formal procedures. In those previous times, it was expected that worshippers accepted a disconnection of the anointed from those in homage. By mid-twentieth century, however, a sense of parity had come into play, in a two-way acknowledgment that priest and parishioners could co-create faith formation. Accordingly, the architectural response was an undivided space for an altar table on a wide platform extending from a back wall to be embraced by surrounding seating that placed the priest and co-celebrants in close relationship with parishioners. Church architecture now became shaped for this new paradigm, with ceilings sloping upward over the altar area as an uplifting gesture of structure.

As parishes guided by their priests took on the job of revising their places of worship to meet Vatican II instructions, the architectural changes had varied outcomes. In most of the older, mainline Gothic-Romanesque churches, principal elements of their architecture remain intact. With removal of the communion rail (in all but a few churches), the altar platform extension with its typical minimally designed altar table, and the resulting rearrangement of pews around the altar platform, constitute the only visible and low-impact change, as the original altar behind and the elaborate reredos continue to display their resplendence. In several churches in rural areas, the changes have resulted in more alterations in the altar and back-pieces within the apse. The overall result is that the change in celebration of services occurs as intended by Vatican II, while original interior architecture is maintained.

## MODERN ARCHITECTURE AS AN INTERPRETER OF FAITH

From a broader viewpoint, the new architecture's shaping of space has mirrored new religious thinking inside and outside of Catholicism concerning a primary tenet of faith. Modern physics sketched out the celestial domain in a highly abstract framework, evolving away from historical principles of heaven as a more physical setting. Modern architects likewise drew designs of churches creating a geometry in which lines and shapes themselves form the beauty of architecture, evoking in parishioners a somewhat abstract aesthetic and faith-fulfilling experience. And reaching to the abstract realms implies long-distance divine communication.

Meanwhile, the older Gothic-Romanesque edifices, their hierarchies of tangible ornament, stained-glass windows and statuary remain in place to give worshippers direct translations of faith-based allegories and lesson plans in the Catholic tradition. And in the larger churches with higher vaulted ceilings, the plaster is tinted with a sky-like blue to assure that the firmament is just above, making a dial-up to the almighty a local call.

PART ONE
# The Early Churches
1871-1930

The earliest permanent Catholic church built in Stearns County was completed in 1871. As of the writing of this book, the latest date of Catholic church construction is 2000. Within that 129-year span, the county has experienced significant changes that have influenced its history. The design of these churches, as this book portrays, instructs us how styles emerge, develop and shift to new architectural expressions in a voluble response to cultural and economic transitions.

Early churches are those built within the tradition of Gothic-Romanesque styles, which begin with churches that are relatively pure Gothic, later influenced by a mix of Gothic and Romanesque, and ending with structures that possess traces of that combined style although mainly clothed in emerging eclectic styles in the early Twentieth Century. In other words, churches with an emblematic tall slender steeple fit within the early church category.

Early churches may also be classified, in a very general sense, as those built by parishes whose members were part of the immigrant generations, meaning these parishioners' lives were within the life spans of the first generation of settlement founders, thus sharing to some degree the immigrant culture that became formative in establishing immigrant-based development patterns.

The earliest of the Catholic churches were built soon after immigrant settlement broke prairie ground, in the rudimentary fashion for temporary use that these circumstances presented. Permanent brick structures were closely patterned after Old Country churches that were still patterning the lives of these immigrant builders, and this Gothic influence set the prototype for the first generation of Catholic churches. In the later years of the nineteenth century, church design began to follow evolving trends in northern Europe that was absorbing the shift to the Romanesque style, that became a hybrid with Gothic in a way that fused the salient features of both styles into church structure and form.

In these years before the twentieth century, American life continued European patterns. The broad spectrum of American architecture reflected this influence, rural areas in particular, and most notably in Stearns County with the northern European cultural insistence on tradition. In this manner, Stearns County Catholic churches in the late nineteenth century bore striking resemblance in general architectural form and detail to northern German rural places of worship reaching back into the Middle Ages.

The early years of the twentieth century across the nation were a continuation of the preceding nineteenth century, but the years after World War I resulted in an economic and technological shift, inducing cultural changes similar in transformational aspect to what was later to occur in America's post World War II period. In Stearns County, the early 1920s saw immigrant influence make way for the generational changes of native-born people, who continued the strong farm way of life while America was beginning its epochal development into urban patterns. The preponderant agrarian way of life came into balance with growth of cities and towns.

In this period of change, architecture changed as well. The Gothic standard for design of cultural institutional buildings in cities and places of worship in rural areas experienced great decline. In Stearns County, the Romanesque style grew in importance from its nineteenth-century alliance with Gothic, then experienced a particular revival in rediscovery of early Christian era basilica forms, some re-using Byzantine expression, that preceded the Middle Ages Gothic domination. All the while, ornament became less useful, as modern ideas came into play.

# ALBANY
# Church of the Seven Dolors

Architect: Erhard Brielmeier, Milwaukee
Contractor: Paul Koshiol, St. Cloud
1889-1899

## PARISH HISTORY

The spire of the Church of Seven Dolors dominates the skyline of Albany in central Stearns County along I-94. It is surrounded by a newly constructed parish center, a rectory, an elementary school, and a nursing home.

The roots of this parish go back to 1863 when the first German settlers arrived in the area by way of Appleton, Wisconsin. Their settlement was called Two Rivers and was located less than a mile southeast of the present church. In the early years, the pioneer families concentrated on clearing the land and building shelters, so religious services were infrequent. The first mass at Two Rivers took place in the home of John Schwinghammer in 1866. Over the next two years the families attended church in parishes that had been established earlier in St. Joseph, fourteen miles to the east, or New Munich, ten miles to the west. This was no small feat considering the fact that they either walked or used a team of oxen and a cart to traverse the long distance to and from mass.

In 1868 the parish was officially organized, and in the same year a log church measuring thirty by twenty feet was built. This structure served the parish for the next four years. An important event in the growth and development of the area took place in 1871 when the St. Paul, Minneapolis, and Manitoba Railroad purchased land and built a depot north of the Two Rivers settlement which they named Albany. A number of businesses followed, and in 1872 a new frame church was built in Albany on land donated by one of the parishioners, Joseph Zeis. The parish grew quickly and by 1889 the church had become too small, and a sixty-by-sixty-five-foot addition was built.

By the late 1890s the parish needed additional space, and noted Milwaukee architect Erhard Brielmeier was hired to draw up the plans. The old part of the church was moved away, and the addition of the new wing made the church cruciform in design. The dedication of the new church took place on August 5, 1900.

An interesting story surrounds the naming of the parish. According to local historians, Simon Groetsch was digging a well on his farm, just north of Albany and sending dirt to the surface by means of a bucket and pulley operated by a family member. After a full bucket had been raised to the surface, the rope slipped, sending the bucket down the shaft towards Simon. Envisioning instant death, he called to the Sorrowful Mother, and the bucket stopped inches from his head. Apparently, the speedy unwinding of the rope had caused it to become entangled, thus saving his life. In thanks for this intercession, Groetsch donated a statue of the Seven Dolors (Sorrows) which was brought from Germany by friends and later placed in the church.

## ARCHITECTURAL DESCRIPTION

If any church in Stearns County can achieve the term "mega-church" it is the Church of the Seven Dolors in Albany. From its large floor plan, a noble yet graceful red-brick structure gives it a size almost unequalled by any church throughout rural Minnesota.

Besides serving as a place of worship for most of the twentieth century and beyond, the Church of the Seven Dolors forms a landmark for travelers along I-94. It is easily seen when passing the town of Albany.

Built in 1872 to 1900, the church's architectural style combines Romanesque and Gothic features on the exterior. The sense of massiveness, accented by corbelled brickwork at the tops of walls, stone-edged gabled parapets rising above roof surfaces are identifying elements of Romanesque, while the use of details typical of Gothic architecture render a delicate character. The church's most prominent Gothic feature is the tall square-based bell tower that supports a slender octagonal spire, perhaps the tallest architectural feature for many miles around.

A recent addition to the building to provide for ancillary parish activities provides a general fit with Seven Dolor's traditional architecture.

The church's interior, one of the largest in Stearns County, consists of a tall nave space with a curved vaulted ceiling intersected by an unusually wide transept that delivers warm magnitudes of light through its large-sized stained glass windows. The main nave walls receive support by large well-spaced columns that demarcate the main nave seating from side aisle seating that is wider than typical churches in the region. This allows the columns to stand a greater than usual distance from the side walls, giving the columns, augmented by the wide arches they support, a prominent role in interior spatial composition. The central high nave gains emphasis of its height by the lower ceiling of the side aisle intersecting vaults. The arch ribs delineate the edges of these curved shapes as well as organize the profusion of surface ornament all around.

The two side aisles are given exquisite terminus by large intensely ornamented altars. The main altar has a likewise intricate wood reredos. Furthering the wide-ranging array of large and tiny design elements are the large stained-glass windows in the nave side walls depicting gospel scenes in rich colors. Corinthian-inspired column capitals have tightly ornamented florid design features.

The total effect of Seven Dolors is composition of perfectly-proportioned space and form. Bold structural features of the high nave ceiling of intersecting vaults lofted above prominent colonnades give a sense of architectural power and celestial majesty so effectively enriched by color and ornament, and amplified by the inherent logic of Gothic structure. They render the Church of the Seven Dolors a sensuous banquet of elaborated details, a magnificent work of religious architecture.

# Avon
# Church of St. Benedict

Architect: Gilbert Winkelmann, OSB, Collegeville
Builder: Paul Pappenfus, St. Cloud
1928

## Parish History

The community of Avon, located in central Stearns County along I-94, is surrounded by rolling hills and numerous lakes and streams. Originally the area was inhabited by Native Americans, and the name given to the original settlement was Spunk Lake after a local Indian chief. The first white settlers, Nicholas and John Keppers, arrived in 1858, bought land and were soon fol-

lowed by several other families. By 1869 the small settlement numbered ten families, who petitioned the Benedictine Abbey at nearby Collegeville for a priest to serve their spiritual needs. The abbey sent Father Benedict Haindl who offered mass on a monthly basis in Nicholas Keppers's wagon shop and later in the log schoolhouse which was built in 1871. The original name for the church was Immaculate Conception, and this was later changed to St. Benedict's, probably in honor of Father Haindl, the priest who had founded the parish.

The arrival of the railroad spurred growth in the area, and the town was renamed Avon. In 1876 planning started on a church which would accommodate increasing numbers of Catholics in the area. The frame church, measuring seventy-six by thirty-four feet was completed in 1878 and was used for fifty years until the present Romanesque basilica structure was built in 1928. The new church was designed by Father Gilbert Winkelmann from St. John's University and measured 144 by sixty-two feet. Much of the labor, including excavation of the basement, was donated by the parishioners.

## ARCHITECTURAL DESCRIPTION

The Church of Saint Benedict is one of three Catholic places of worship in Stearns County built in the original basilica style that originated in pre-Christian times and evolved into third and fourth century to be known as the Romanesque style. Unlike Gothic edifices that incorporate a cruciform floor plan by means of transepts (short extensions from the rectangular nave near the sanctuary), the side walls of Saint Benedict's nave run straight their entire length. A large addition on the front façade of the church carries similar materials and details.

The exterior's architectural expression of the early Romanesque is seen in its medium-pitched clay tiled roof stepped back for the upper clerestory nave walls, a sizeable bell tower set into the corner of the façade, and narrow windows with geometrical patterned tinted glass in consistent-sized bands across the façade and along the nave.

In the interior, Saint Benedict follows the basilica plan of the early Romanesque style with plain-faced brick regularly spaced piers with slightly elaborated brick patterns at top and bottom surfaces. Plaster-clad beams above the piers contain cornices with simply elaborated continuously curved moldings, which provide a distinct separation between the upper clerestory walls and the lower supporting structure. Flat beams set on simple curvilinear brackets support the roof.

A modest granite altar in the spirit of Vatican II stands before a simple baldachin containing basic classical details Side aisles have whose roof sets below the clerestory walls have arched ceilings. With its elementary details set into a relatively small-scaled structure, Saint Benedict ably contributes to the architecture of Stearns County.

# COLLEGEVILLE
# Church of
# St. John the Baptist

Organized: 1875

The parish of St. John the Baptist in Collegeville, just west of St. Joseph, is unique in that it has never built a church of its own. Members attend mass in the Assumption Chapel in the lower level of the Abbey Church at St. John's University.

When the Benedictine priests moved from St. Cloud to establish an abbey and monastery in what is now Collegeville, they invited the local settlers to attend mass in a small chapel at the monastery. Most of the settlers, who had established farms nearby, had previously been part of the parish in St. Joseph. In 1875 a petition to start their own parish was signed by the heads of eighteen families. Permission was quickly given and Benedictine Father Clement Staub became their first pastor in 1876.

Over the years the relationship of the parish to the abbey has been strong, and when the Abbey Church was built in 1961, the parish donated the Baptismal font near the entrance.

In the early 1980s, seeking to have its own identity, the congregation made plans to build a parish center adjacent to the university campus. When estimates came in for the project, it became clear that the cost exceeded their budget. Undaunted, several parishioners experienced in construction stepped forward, and along with donations of materials and equipment, were able to complete the center at a cost that was much lower than estimates.

In recent years, the center has been the scene of monthly Sunday brunches, which attract people from a large area, and serve as the main fundraiser for the parish.

# EDEN VALLEY
# Church of the Assumption

Architect and builder: Unknown
1894–1937

## PARISH HISTORY

The town of Eden Valley lies within two counties, Stearns and Meeker, and at one time had two Catholic churches located only five blocks apart. The Assumption parish founded by German settlers was established in 1892 succeeding a church in a nearby settlement called Logering which closed after the Soo Line railroad bypassed it and laid tracks through Eden Valley. The first masses in Eden Valley were held in a hall above the local butcher shop in 1892, and the rapid growth necessitated the building of a permanent church. In 1894 the present brick church measuring forty-two by seventy feet was dedicated.

By 1904 Irish immigrants in the area had received permission to start a parish, and their church, St. Peter's, was built just south of Assumption in the Meeker County side of town. Over the years, the decline in membership at St. Peter's, along with the shortage of priests forced a decision to merge with the Assumption parish. This process was done gradually by combining religious instruction and parish groups over a ten-year period. The two parishes became one on July 1, 1999.

41

The Assumption church has undergone several renovations over the years, the biggest of which was the addition of two wings in 1937. Additional space for the sacristy was added in the 1960s.

## ARCHITECTURAL DESCRIPTION

The Church of the Assumption assumes the traditional tall square bell tower set into the center of its façade, clothed in red-orangish-beige brick. The tower's relatively short cap may indicate replacement of an original, much-higher, pointed spire. On each side of the bell tower, pair of tall Gothic arch windows, with a small round window above, are crowned by an elaborate series of corbels whose lower tips create a gable form in the façade face that frame the windows—a sensitive design that becomes the façade's distinguishing feature. A horizontal band with a pair of slightly projecting brick courses gives a subtle articulation that brick is so adept at providing.

The main section of the ceiling of the Church of the Assumption has a dominant array of large dark-stained wood arches supporting a steeply pitched ceiling. Crisscrossing angled members are connected by thick vertical struts,

scroll-cut to form openings in the shape of arched window openings—a motif also used at the Church of Saint Joseph in Waite Park. In the transept part of the nave that was built in 1937, the wood trusses take on more slender profiles while achieving complimenting configuration.

The main nave walls contain Gothic arched stained-glass windows, each with a circle in the upper section displaying a liturgical symbol that is part of the traditional symbolism in Catholic church history, set in a background of intertwining ovals in pale tones of yellow and beige. The transept's stained-glass windows are shaped by American interpretations of Tudor architectural features. A low-pitched, pointed arch window head contains a series of six vertical sashes holding rectangular glazing panels. Randomly placed angled muntins separate contrasting colors predominated by blues and green along with occasional reds, with the total effect being a lively abstract pattern.

Within the sanctuary's white-walled enclosure, a back altar three-part panel presents hand-carved wood rich in intricate patterns of vertical moldings which frame circular and intertwining patterns. The altar facing uses three panels with tri-partite arch patterns. Above the back altar, the center and much wider panel gives prominence to a crucifix with gild-tipped edges, set underneath an arch composed of Gothic-Revival-infused tracery.

# ELROSA
# Church of
# Sts. Peter and Paul

Architect: Leo Schaefer, St. Cloud
Builder: Albert Kind, St. Cloud
1917-1925

## PARISH HISTORY

By 1857, the area around the present town of Elrosa had been settled by over thirty families, and in that same year, Benedictine Father Clement Staub said

mass in the home of the first families. Unlike most of the other settlements, where parishes were formed and churches built in a very short period of time, this parish was not officially organized until 1889. In those intervening years, most of the families attended church in Spring Hill.

The parish built its first frame church in 1891 in Lake George, a small settlement a few miles south of the present town of Elrosa. Two parishioners, Joseph Heinze, Sr., and his son, Joseph Heinze, Jr., both skilled craftsmen, supervised the project. In 1908 the Soo Line Railroad laid tracks a few miles north of the original settlement, and the ensuing growth there eventually led to the demise of the Lake George settlement. In 1914 the parish built a rectory in Elrosa that contained a small chapel where mass could be offered, but

regular services continued at the Lake George church until 1917 when the basement portion for a new church in Elrosa had been completed. The Lake George church was dismantled in the same year; the lumber was saved, and in 1918 was used to build a social hall for the parish.

Construction on the superstructure of the new Spanish Basilica style church began in 1925, and the completed church was dedicated on July 6, 1926.

The town of Elrosa received its name in an interesting way. The land for the railroad right of way was purchased from Lewis Michels, an early settler. When a representative from the railroad approached the family about naming the town, it was decided to reverse the first two letters of Lewis, then add the name of his daughter Rosa, thus Elrosa.

## ARCHITECTURAL DESCRIPTION

Located in the small agricultural community in western Stearns County, the Church of Saints Peter and Paul represents the second decade of the twentieth century continuing a shift from the omni-present Gothic-Romanesque style prevalent in the 1880s to revivals of later German origin. The architecture of Saints Peter and Paul is based on German Baroque with Spanish influences. The brick façade is an asymmetrical composition composed of a somewhat narrow gable centered between a tall prominent bell tower supporting a copper clad dome at the northwest corner and a much shorter flat-roofed tower and the southwest corner. The main entrance features a slightly projecting stone arched doorway that frames a pair of doors. Above, a round rose window in the upper part of the gable form, which is topped by a shallow-pitched para-pet notched close to each end to form small flat parapet corners. Windows in the façade show subtle influences of the emerging Colonial Revival style that also appears on a few other Stearns County churches built during this time in the vicinity of Saints Peter and Paul.

Saints Peter and Paul's interior follows the design of fourth century Roman basilicas that were more basic in layout before the Gothic period employed them as a template for that style's structural acrobatics. In this church, simple arcades set away from and parallel to nave side walls support upper clerestory walls that carry a shallow curved ceiling vault across the cen-tral nave space. A continuous band with a slight projection top and a repeat-ing leaf pattern extends along the lower section of the clerestory wall. Side windows, nearly square in shape with segmented arch heads, contain stained glass images of saints against an intertwining geometrical background.

The altar is a simple table with a draped cloth cover. A small taberna-cle enclosure stands in back of the altar below a simplified wall-hung slight-ly projecting arched canopy. On the curved wall of the apse is a painted Christ child and Mary with a gold halo.

Austere · Subdued · Subtle

# Farming
# Church of St. Catherine

Architect: Unknown
Builder: A.G. Wahl, St. Cloud
1903

## Parish History

The first settlers reached the Farming area as early as 1858, coming from several regions in Germany including Westphalia, Hanover, and Oldenburg. They came to Stearns County with the hope of owning their own land, which had

become impossible in their native country. Farming township was organized in 1873, and a small village sprung up which was never incorporated.

In 1879 thirty families met with the intention of building their own church. Up to this time, they had to travel to Richmond, seven miles away, to attend services. Permission was granted by the bishop, and in June of 1881, a simple frame church was dedicated on land donated by Michael Bock. The joy of having their own church was short-lived, however, when a tornado completely destroyed it a few months after its completion. The

parishioners rebuilt at a cost of $2,400, and it was blessed in November of 1902. On February 16, 1903, this church burned to the ground. With great sacrifice, the parishioners met with the intention of building a much larger brick church. Work was started in June of 1903, and the completed church was dedicated in December of the same year. Between 1909 and 1912 the interior was remodeled using the altars, pews, pulpit, and communion rails from the old Abbey Church at St. John's University. Stained glass windows were added in 1912.

## ARCHITECTURAL DESCRIPTION

Saint Catherine Catholic Church follows the exterior patterns of Stearns County Catholic churches—brick walls on a stone foundation, steep-pitched roof with a bell tower slightly projecting from the center of the façade, with an arched main entrance. Brick corbelling of Romanesque derivation appears in somewhat subdued form, stepping with façade roof edges and running along tops of nave walls. The church's architecture is not firmly set within any particular style; it combines the traditional Stearns church building type clothed in a generalized Colonial Revival form with traces of Romanesque.

Saint Catherine's nave is a simple barrel vault, performing a clear span from side wall to side wall, a continuous curved shape from façade to sanctuary. The vault surface is clad with twelve-by-twenty-four-inch acoustic tile panels, a material that originated in the 1950s, undoubted added since original construction. The sanctuary is divided from the nave by a flat wall with an arched opening leading to the sanctuary, rendering a sense of separation unlike

typical nineteenth-century Stearns County churches. The principal feature of this relatively simple space are the tall stained-glass windows, half-round arched heads, with glass panels depicting figures of the saints, females on the left wall and males on the right wall. Also on the right wall is a wood mission cross. Large stations of the cross panels are aligned on the side walls, and a noticeable aspect is the text in German rather than the more typical English in most other Stearns County churches.

The original altar, as in almost all Stearns County churches, has a facing that is a series of arches tipped with gold paint. The back altarpiece features Gothic-like tall vertical open-faced enclosures—a statue of Christ in the center chamber with female figures within smaller chambers on each side.

Saint Catherine's architectural design in 1903 displays the evolving progression away from the conspicuous ornamentation and elaborated structure of the nineteenth-century Gothic towards an architectural austerity marked by simpler structure and reduction of ornament. As in other Stearns County Catholic churches of this early twentieth-century era, the beauty of Saint Catherine's is austerity surpassed by subtle enrichment. Architecture here is non-dependent on amplitude of ornament but on ornament's location—designed so its placement on simple surfaces can allow its aesthetic forming religious intention to show forth.

FREEPORT

# Church of the Sacred Heart

Architects: Parkinson and Dockendorff, La Crosse
Builder: Paul Koshiol, St. Cloud
1905-1913

## PARISH HISTORY

The early settlement of Freeport began in the 1860s, and the town was originally called Oak Station. Before the Sacred Heart parish was formed, the settlers attended church in the nearby towns of St. Anthony, Albany, and New Munich. In 1881 a group petitioned the bishop of the vicariate in St. Cloud to

send a priest to their area. Father Simplicius Wimmer, a Benedictine from St. John's Abbey, became the first priest to say mass in the settlement; the parish is still served by the Benedictines.

Their first church, a wood-frame structure measuring twenty-two by seventy feet, was dedicated in 1882. Within a few years, the parish had grown to 175 families, and it became apparent that a much larger church would be needed. The second church, a brick-and-stone structure measuring 154 by sixty-six feet and seating nearly 1,000 people, was built in 1896, and dedicated by Bishop Trobec in 1898. The original church was moved to St. Rosa, about five miles away. It was later brick veneered and remodeled, and is still in use today.

On October 12, 1904, a fire of unknown origin completely destroyed the second church. Planning began immediately for a new church, and by 1906 the exterior was completed.

A committee of parishioners then began the process of fundraising to complete the interior. Records show that great care was taken in the selection of materials and craftsmen for the project. The back and side altars were finished in 1910 followed by the stained-glass windows in 1911. By the time all the interior furnishing had been completed in 1913, total cost of the church had risen to $115,000.

## ARCHITECTURAL DESCRIPTION

Approaching the town of Freeport from Interstate I-94, this Gothic style church appears somewhat diminutive, and this perception persists in approaching the building's modest façade. But after passing through the

small-scaled vestibule, the nave expresses an enormous expanding feeling of space, especially in its verticality, with its complex series of Gothic arches demarcated with ribbed edges, all creating a special airiness with a complex of curved intersecting vaults, tinted soft blue that hints of the ethereal.

Sacred Heart was designed by Parkinson and Dockendorff Architects of LaCrosse, Wisconsin. In his book Churches of Minnesota, Alan K. Lathrop notes that thirty-eight boxcar loads of bricks were needed to construct the church, and the main and side altars were made by the Deprato Statuary Company of New York, and the stained glass windows were fabricated by Ford Brothers Glass Company of Minneapolis. Lathrop also remarks in 1911, parishioners installed a clock in the steeple that operates by an elaborate system of pulleys and weights, requiring hand pulls on a chain once a day, that runs flawlessly today.

Sacred Heart was built with a cruciform floor plan. Saint Cloud beige brick walls on a rough-faced Mankato sandstone foundation give form to some-what modest architectural details based on both Gothic and Romanesque Revival styles. The church's symmetry is expressed in a dominant square steeple centered in the façade. Just above the roof ridge line, the square steeple becomes octagonal, each face having a tall narrow Gothic pointed arch louver-infilled opening, leading upward to diminutive outfacing gables that seem to brace the tall pointed spire. The exterior of the nave walls displays

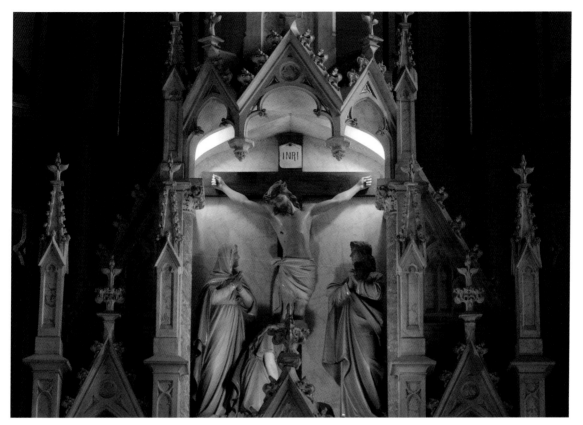

Gothic pointed arch windows demarcated by buttresses, with Romanesque Revival brick corbelling in arch motif patterns running the length of the top of the nave walls.

Sacred Heart's straightforward exterior contrasts its intricate interior. A spacious transept in the forward part of the nave amplifies the complex delicacy of space. The sanctuary's most eye-arresting feature is the half-octagonal apse whose verticality is accentuated with narrow bays that taper to a small flat circle that joins the apse vault ribs. The bay's flat panels feature quatrefoil emblems whose centers contain angel-winged heads, an eagle, a lion, a bull, and a human baby, with sacred heart motifs flanking the altar. An inscription on an archway leading to the sanctuary reads: *"Sieh da dieses Herz, das die Menschen so sehr geliebt hat."* ("Behold this Heart, that has loved mankind so much.")

In the middle of the sanctuary, an elaborate altar ensemble structured in white marble reaches upward, composed of Gothic arched gable pediments in tripartite shapes with almost confectionary ornamental details. The altar is built of marble, with its base face featuring three panels, the center being the largest with a carved relief of the Last Supper in which polychrome figures surround Christ in frozen animation.

In these Gothic churches of Stearns County, the slender structural network creating uplifting spatial wonder becomes enriched by a seemingly inexhaustible array of ornament found in columns, brackets, and articulated wall surfaces, but special focal points are the stained-glass windows. Centered in each nave bay, their Gothic arched tops form a framework for two pointed arched stained-glass panels surmounted by a circular panel just under the top of the frame. These large assemblies are made from thousands of stained glass pieces in bright and muted colors. The pattern of using stained-glass windows —the left side (facing the altar) depicting scenes from the Old Testament and the right side using the New Testament is prevalent throughout Europe, and Sacred Heart is a terrific example—possibly the best in Stearns County. The symbols of the faith: Old Testament motifs such as Noah's ark are on the left side, and the wheat and vines, saints, and other symbols in the New Testament appear on the right side.

The Stations of the Cross at Sacred Heart are works of art in themselves. Mounted on the side walls of the aisles, this carved stone statuary is set in architectural frames, with figures in dramatic poses accentuated with polychrome, expressing anguish and pain in the manner of Renaissance paintings.

Listed on the National Register of Historic Places, Sacred Heart commits to the fullest extent possible to its role as a well-architecturally orchestrated representation of regional religious architecture.

# HOLDINGFORD
# Church of St. Mary
Architect and Builder : Unknown
1914

## PARISH HISTORY

Unlike most of the rural settlements in Stearns County in the latter half of the nineteenth century, Holdingford was multi-ethnic, composed of Irish, Scotch, German and Polish people. The first settlers, mostly Irish, arrived in the late 1870s, and the first masses were held in the homes of local citizens and at the schoolhouse. By 1885, St. Mary's parish had been established, and plans made for a church.

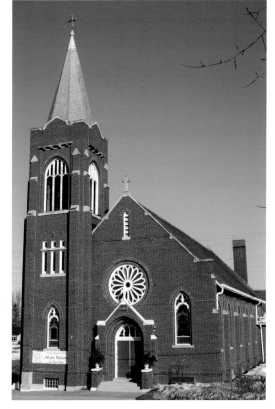

Money was scarce, and the prospects for building a church were dim until three parishioners cooperated in the donation of land. Anton Vos, Sr., John Muyres, Sr., and Reinhard Vos stipulated that their donated land should be used for a church, rectory, cemetery, and pasture for the pastor's horse. Father Xavier White, St. Mary's first pastor, then devised a way to get the church built without a great deal of cash. He visited the parishioners and asked them to donate logs, which were made into lumber at the local sawmill at no charge to the parish. Construction of the frame church began in the spring of 1886 and was finished the same year. The rectory was completed in 1889.

By 1910 the Polish population of the area had increased greatly, and they decided to form their own parish, St.

Hedwig's. Despite the drop in numbers at St. Mary's, the parish continued to flourish, and in 1915, the present church was completed at a location about one mile east of the original frame church.

## ARCHITECTURAL DESCRIPTION

The Church of Saint Mary's red-brick Gothic façade rises up from the sidewalk along one of Holdingford's main streets, with a sizeable corner bell tower. Tower faces in its upper section have large openings without enclosing louvered panels that are typical of Gothic bell towers. The church's main entrance features a recessed doorway leading to a small vestibule.

Saint Mary's interior departs from the typical Gothic arched ceiling; instead a central flat panel flanked by flat sloping panels forms the nave ceiling, edged with wood molding giving subtle detail to the church's interior. A shallow-crowned arch separates the nave from the sanctuary, which holds a profusely detailed reredo, built of varnished wood similar to many others in the county, but given liveliness here with multicolored detail.

The stairway to the choir loft is quite narrow, with winding treads, but the climb is worth the effort, as peering from the choir loft, Saint Mary's offers a sense of expanded depth and volume. In the stairwell are hanging ropes leading downward from a small ceiling area that undoubtedly toll the bells that peal out to the townspeople of Holdingford.

## HOLDINGFORD
# Church of St. Hedwig
Architect: Charles Shand
Builder: Val Herman
1910

### PARISH HISTORY

On April 10, 1910 a group of Polish Catholics, who had been attending the predominately German St. Mary's parish in Holdingford, met with the purpose of establishing their own parish and building a church. The main reason for this initiative was probably so that the sermons and sacraments could be

delivered in their native language. They also knew that Polish churches had been started in recent years in nearby Opole and St. Anna, and that there were Polish priests who would be available to serve them. At the initial meeting, under the leadership of Father Peter Brenny, the parish was formed with the name St. Hedwig's, land was purchased, and the decision was made to go forward with plans to build a church. At a meeting a week later, the parish was incorporated, and Father Brenny was named the first pastor.

In October of the same year, Bishop Trobec laid the cornerstone, and the completed church was blessed the following fall. In the ensuing years, the new parish achieved a great deal of stability due to an increase in the number of families and the long tenure of one of its first pastors, Father Golkowski, who served St. Hedwig's from 1911 until 1923. At the present time, both Catholic parishes in Holdingford, lying only a few blocks apart, are served by the same priest.

## ARCHITECTURAL DESCRIPTION

The Church of Saint Hedwig is one of several in Stearns County that represents the transition in architectural styles from Gothic to Romanesque that occurred in the nation and throughout Stearns County in the early decades of the twentieth century. The front façade is characterized by a traditional feature of Gothic architecture: steep pitched roof whose gable is intersected by a tall square shaft of the bell tower, stepping back slightly as it rises, capped with a steep faceted spire. The nave walls show slightly engaged pilasters that likewise step in slightly while reaching upwards, and the pointed arched windows set between the pilasters are typical Gothic elements. The Romanesque style melds effortlessly into Saint Hedwig's architecture, with red brick instead of the German Gothic beige-yellow, corbelled tops of nave walls and the gables extending above roof planes that are capped with stone trim.

The Church of Saint Hedwig represents the Polish emigrants' choice for a nave of more straightforward shape. The floor plan, uninterrupted by colonnades separating side aisles from the centered nave space in the Gothic fashion, is covered by a clear span curved vaulted ceiling. The side walls of the nave feature stained-glass windows whose heads reach just below the curved base of the vaulted ceiling.

The sanctuary provides a departure from the Gothic, dispensing the semi-circular of half-octagonal apse to be replaced by a somewhat shallow arched recess with a flat wall behind, giving cover to the altar and its heavily elaborate back piece. Here the intricate thicket of the Gothic reredo gives way to a center half-open chamber immediately above the altar, serving to showcase a large crucifix. The front of the chamber is bordered by ornate columns that support a half-hexagonal canopy encrusted in gilded detail. On each side, smaller chambers repeat the sanctuary arched enclosure with shallow arched recesses that hold statues of saints. This background structure is mounted to the top and back of the altar, and its wood surfaces are painted in white, with gold edging of the copious detail and blue emblem-like panels.

The overall architectural character of this interior renders a feeling of simplicity, resulting from a ceiling that is lower than Gothic churches, but a more intimate sense of space is achieved with well-placed intricate detail that both contrasts and balances its spatial envelope.

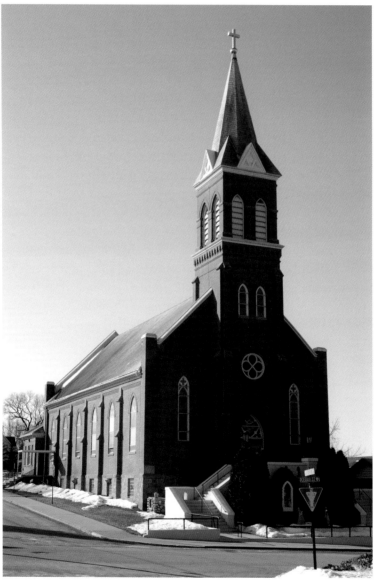

## Jacob's Prairie
# Church of St. James
Builders: Hennen Brothers Lumber and congregation built
1930

### Parish History

This picturesque stone-and-granite church is located in the small hamlet of Jacob's Prairie between St. Joseph and Cold Spring. St. James is one of the oldest parishes in the county, founded by Father Pierz, who was known to have visited the area in 1854 to say mass in the homes of the earliest settlers.

In 1856 Father Pierz related in a letter that he had, "acquired in St. Jacob ten acres of good land." A log church was built in the same year and was used by the settlers until it burned down two years later. Benedictine priests took charge of the congregation from the beginning, coming at irregular intervals to say mass and perform the sacraments until a resident pastor was appointed in 1873.

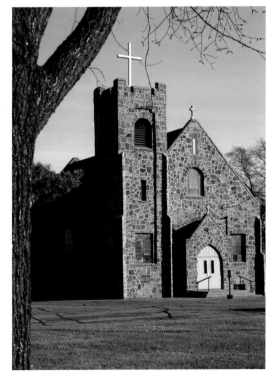

Throughout the years, the people have shown great faith and resolve through trying times to maintain their parish. The grasshopper infestations of 1856 and 1875 devastated crops, and new parishes were formed in nearby Cold Spring and St. Nicholas, taking members from their congregation. When a tornado destroyed their second church in 1894, there was talk of dissolving their small parish, but the settlers persisted, and permission was granted to rebuild. In 1930 a fire destroyed this church, and again pledges of money and labor were responsible for the construction of the present church, which was dedicated in 1931.

## Architectural Description

The architectural inventory of Catholic churches of rural immigrant origins in Stearns County encompasses over forty churches built in a six-decade time span. That period began with the Gothic-Romanesque style directly transplanted from Northern regions of Germany, a style that dominated Stearns County rural Catholic church architecture, through most of that time. However, the second decade of the twentieth century presented social and religious forces for which the style gradually became obsolescent, as Gothic architectural elements increasing played a lesser role.

The architecture of Saint James represents a house of worship in which Gothic-style features are virtually absent. The church's massing provides a handsome composition without the verticality typical of Gothic churches. Windows in nave walls and in the lower façade section have square tops—a hint of Modernity to come—in lieu of the obligatory pointed or round arch tops of Gothic and Romanesque.

The façade's steep gable reaches a modest height, with the corner bell tower giving the composition a well-proportioned vertical offset. The bell tower's flat roof is a noticeable shift away from the pointed spires of preceding Stearns County Catholic churches. The entire exterior is enriched by stone walls laid in random pattern with relatively wide mortar joints, whose whitish color accentuates the lively mix of the color range of the stone.

The interior has an open, mildly modern feeling, consisting of a simple floor plan, a ceiling supported by a series of wood trusses whose design is characterized by bold members and prominent openings between. The altar area has a simple floor rectangular floor plan with a straightforward gable ceiling. The altar is an uncomplicated table; behind is a ceiling-hung crucifix.

# Lake Henry
# Church of St. Margaret

Architect: Herman Gaul, Chicago
Builder: Kropp and Sons, St. Cloud
1922

## Parish History

The settlement of the area around what is now Lake Henry began in the early 1850s, and Father Pierz is said to have visited there in 1855. Over the next twenty-five years, various Benedictine missionaries visited the area and said mass in the homes of families. Services were infrequent. When mass was not offered in Lake Henry, settlers attended mass in Spring Hill and St. Martin.

In 1880 a group met at the home of Michael Kraemer, Sr., to organize a parish. Permission was granted by Bishop Seidenbusch, and by 1881, their first church, a wood-frame structure measuring fifty by thirty-six feet was built. The original name of the parish was St. Rupert's, and later changed to St. Margaret's, in honor Michael Kraemer's wife. Over the next five years, as the parish grew, the church was enlarged, and a bell tower was added. In 1886 a school was built and staffed by Benedictine sisters from St. Joseph.

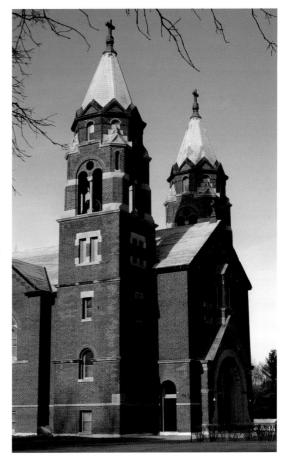

Father Joseph Linz became pastor in 1918 and served the parish until his retirement in 1955, and it was under his leadership that plans were made for the present church. A campaign was initiated to raise funds, and with pledges of donated labor from the men of the parish, construction started in 1922. The new twin-towered church was dedicated in 1923. Because of the Depression, much of the interior work had to be postponed. It wasn't until 1941 that the stained-glass windows were installed. These windows are the most distinctive feature of the church interior.

## ARCHITECTURAL DESCRIPTION

The architecture of the Church of Saint Margaret's exhibits its distinct Romanesque style in which walls with more concentrated window openings, giving more expanses of brick, lend a sense of solidity characteristic of that style, along with more pronounced round arched windows and wide semi-circular arches with distinct stone edging. The continuing shift from the once-prevalent Gothic style can be seen in the moderate slope of the main roof and substantial bell towers with spires of greater girth and not so steep roof slopes. Moreover, the Romanesque character is further emboldened by the façade's main gable projecting forward from the side bell towers, rather than inset in the mode of Gothic churches.

The interior features an elongated half-circular vaulting across the relatively wide nave. Saint Margaret's distinctive feature is the nave side walls having shallow transept-like off-set walls with large gable faces emphasized with expansive three-part stained glass windows, repeated towards the sanctuary with a much deeper and wider transept, with even larger stained glass windows in the upper gables.

Typical of the Vatican II reform, the altar table is a simple object in the space of the altar platform, and the rear wall is an assembly of wood panels with

a slightly recessed arch containing a crucifix. The interior architectural components express the heavy proportions of the Romanesque, but the slightly creamy surfaces seem to absorb the predominant reds and blues of the light-infused stained glass, creating an overall sense of warmth and comfort.

## LUXEMBURG
# Church of St. Wendelin
Architect: Nicholas Steil
Builder: Unknown
1872

### PARISH HISTORY

St. Wendelin's church, a Gothic style structure made of granite, was completed in 1873 and is still in use today. An elementary school built in 1964 and a parish hall, completed in 1999, serve this parish located eight miles south of St. Cloud on State Highway 15.

Although there is record of settlement in the area going back to 1852, the parish was not officially organized until 1859. In that year, Benedictine missionary priest Father Clement Staub visited the settlement and offered mass in the home of Henry Reding. At the same time, Father Staub urged the settlers to build a church. In a short time $300.00 had been raised, and construction of the first framed church followed. The parish was originally called the Church of All Saints and later named St. Wendelin's in honor of St. Wendelin, a Benedictine abbot who was considered by Germans as the patron of farm people.

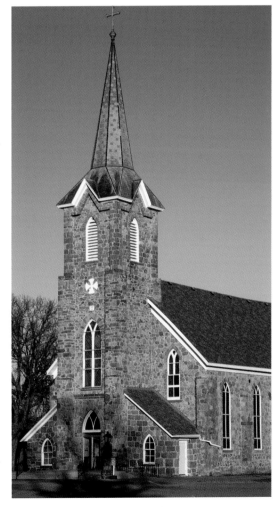

The town which grew up around the church also underwent a change of names. It was originally called St. Wendelin, later becoming West St. Augusta, and finally Luxemburg, after the country of origin of most of the area settlers. By 1871 plans started for the present church, and from the beginning,

the parishioners wanted it to be built of granite which was plentiful in the area. They enlisted Nicolas Steil (later Father Gregory Steil) to draw up the plans. Construction started in May of 1872 with much of the labor, including the cutting of granite blocks, donated by members of the parish. Work proceeded until money ran out in the late summer. At that time, the walls were six feet high, and the steeple had been only partially completed. After additional funds had been raised over the fall and winter, construction resumed, and mass in the completed church was held on Christmas Day in 1873.

## Architectural Description

Saint Wendelin Catholic Church's stone exterior is a notable example of a regional church building built with

local materials. Saint Wendelin's predominately Gothic style reflects relatively early from the date of construction. Granite, quarried nearby and laid in random joints, dominates the building's exterior shell from top to bottom, without major architectural details, except for buttresses on the nave walls and corners of the bell tower, as well as gable-like inset stone panels at the tower's top section that supports the spire.

The nave follows the pattern of Stearns churches in small hamlets that built relatively modest size places of worship. The long front-to-back side of the nave is straight up from ground to roof, without stepped-back clerestory sections.

The vestibule's relatively narrow width makes it more of an entry, with a four-foot-wide pair of doors leading to the nave. Inside the nave, a distinguishing feature of Saint Wendelin is immediately apparent—a double-curved ceiling, referred to as a hammer beam-truss system, a pair of low-sloped curves springing from sidewalls, joined at their edges with a much steeper uprising vault, in a half-trefoil pattern; this unique ceiling running the entire length of the nave. The top vaulted surfaces display oil paintings of various life-of-Christ scenes, probably painted off-site with the canvases attached to the ceiling surfaces. Very narrow and tall stained-glass windows punctuate nave walls, with sunlight washing the plaster of the deep recesses formed by the stone walls' considerable thickness, rendering a pleasant effect to Saint Wendelin's interior. Stations of the Cross are a main feature of the nave's ornamental character,

along with stenciled bands near the top of the walls and around the arched opening between the nave and sanctuary.

The sanctuary is a simple, somewhat narrow space with a flat back wall with a pointed arch ceiling. The plain altar has no reredo. The sacristy, instead of being located at one of the sides of the sanctuary, is in back of the sacristy.

Another feature of the church is a pipe organ in the choir loft, said to have been built in 1845, and considered an instrument of great historic value.

# MARTY
# Church of the Holy Cross
Architect and builder: unknown
1896-1913

## PARISH HISTORY

The Holy Cross parish had its beginnings in 1889 when ten families from the original St. Nicholas church bought land with the intention of building their own church. In their letter of request to the bishop, the families cited overcrowding at St. Nicholas as the reason for needing a new parish. Permission was granted, and a frame church measuring thirty-six by seventy-six feet was soon completed. In the beginning, the parish was called St. Lawrence's and

quickly grew to forty-five families. Services were irregular since only one priest was serving parishes in nearby Jacob's Prairie, Cold Spring, and St. Nicholas as well.

In 1894 the same tornado that had destroyed or damaged so many other churches in the area also struck St. Lawrence's and left it in ruins. The organ was found hanging from a nearby tree. Until the present brick church was built, most of the parishioners attended mass in Luxemburg. The name of the parish was changed to Holy Cross at the time the new church was dedicated in 1896. With the appointment of a resident pastor in 1909, services could be held on a regular basis. In 1913, due to further growth in the area, the church was enlarged by adding two wings making it cruciform in shape. Over the years the church has been remodeled and kept in excellent condition.

## ARCHITECTURAL DESCRIPTION

Located along the main highway route through the hamlet of Marty, the Church of the Holy Cross has yellow brick—a local Stearns County brick—walls, a rectangular bell tower, slightly recessed and centered in the façade. The slender spire rising from a flared roof atop the masonry shaft and the steep main roof that give the building a sense of verticality that indicates its Gothic derivation. The tall and narrow shape of the stained-glass windows in the side

walls of the nave are also Gothic inspired, while their half-circular arch heads represent Romanesque influence.

The nave of Holy Cross presents an interesting interplay of various curving ceiling segments that give shape to much of the interior. The main section of the nave has a flat ceiling center panel that bends downward toward the tops of side walls. Round transept ceilings join the main side curves in crisp splaying arcs. The wall separating the nave and sanctuary contains three half-round arches—the larger center one becomes the open face of the half-round vaulted sanctuary ceiling, with the arches on each side outline shallow niches that face the nave.

The Church of the Holy Cross is similar to several other smaller-scaled Stearns Catholic churches in their non-reliance of ornament to embellish architectural form. Nonetheless, a delicate sense of articulation is delivered by tin-plate ceiling panels whose stamped surfaces emanate circular profuse patterns repeated over all ceiling surfaces. A special feature is the pair of large stained-glass windows in the transept walls, three sections integrated in each arched sash—one with Christ aloft in clouds, the other displays a female saint rising out of what appears to be an open crypt containing a bed of flowers.

The apse's slightly curved wall features few elements—a crucifix, a pair of small round stained-glass windows, and two polychromed (several paint colors applied to plaster figures) statues. Stations of the Cross, likewise polychromed, are larger than those in most other churches, having molded features displaying depth and a vivid sense of portrayal.

# MEIRE GROVE
# Church of
# St. John the Baptist

Architect: Leo Schaefer, St. Cloud
Builders: unknown
1923

## PARISH HISTORY

The first settlers in the Meire Grove area arrived in 1857. They were two brothers, Henry and Xavier Schaefer, who were born in Westphalia and had earlier lived in Iowa before learning of the opportunities available to procure good farming land in Stearns County. They were soon joined by several other families, and in a short time requested a priest to offer mass and the sacraments. Father Clement Staub visited in the fall of 1858 and offered mass on a carpenter's bench in the cabin of the Schaefer brothers.

In 1864, parishioners in Meire Grove built a log church, measuring eighteen feet by thirty feet, unheated with a dirt floor. A Benedictine priests traveling through the area offered mass for this small congregation, as they did for other nearby settlements, at monthly intervals. In 1871, the parish of fifty families, almost all of German origin, built a wood framed church with Gothic style elements, dedicated as the Church of Saint John the Baptist, with local labor and materials hauled in from nearby Melrose. By 1880, the parish had doubled in size, numbering approximately 1,000 persons, and a newly appointed priest, Father Meinulf Stuckenkemper, began the process of fundraising and mobilizing efforts to construct a new and larger church,

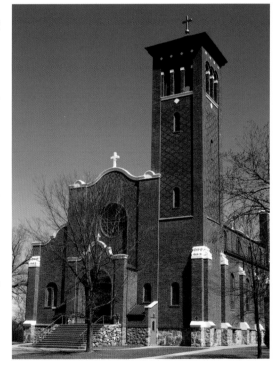

based on his experience in building a church in St. Cloud. All members of the parish were asked to pledge money for the church, and soon enough money had been collected to begin construction. Records show that a donation of 150 marks was received from the Grand Duke of Oldenburg.

Parishioners hauled granite blocks from nearby farm pastures for the foundation. Wagon loads of building material came from the railroad depot in Melrose, and the brick was made by a local brickyard. This church carried much more of the Gothic style, in this case Gothic Revival, undoubtedly due to its St. Cloud architect A.E. Hussey, who was likely influenced by that style's popularity throughout the nation then. Also, the church's size and complexity meant a master mason, John Kropp from St. Cloud, directed a crew of local bricklayers, and a chief carpenter, Carl Lethert, oversaw the structural framing of walls and complex vaulted ceilings as well as the 156-foot high steeple.

Architectural historian Fred W. Peterson noted in his book *Building Community, Keeping the Faith: German Catholic Vernacular Architecture in a Rural Minnesota Parish*, Saint John the Baptist carried a resemblance to the "hallenkirchen (Gothic parish churches) in northwestern German provinces, in particular—the Church of Saints Peter and Paul in Holdorf, Germany. Peterson also writes that during a blizzard on February 13, 1923, a fire completely destroyed the building. The parish immediately began the task of replacement, this time in the modified German Baroque mode, one of the architectural styles coming about in the early twentieth century.

## ARCHITECTURAL DESCRIPTION

St. John the Baptist Church is located within the center of Meire Grove's business area on the east side of the town's main street. The church's principal architectural features a Baroque somewhat asymmetrical façade built with brown brick, characterized by curved-cap stone parapets, with a corner square bell

tower. The entrance is set out from the main façade face, with a semi-circular arched opening leading to an inset entrance with a pair of doors. The church's exterior belongs to the German Baroque style, characterized by its somewhat undulating parapet rising above the gable roof behind it with granite blocks that form column capitals and function to support the spring line of the arches.

The interior features a half-hexagonal-shaped apse clad in glazed yellow brick, layered in running bond with alternating tones of silver-yellow, orange-yellow and beige-yellow, each tone stacked vertically. The vaulted ceiling features a painted Christ head, called a Pantocreator, Coptic-like in two-dimension representation, flanked by two sets of six angel heads with wings. At the base of the vault, a band of marching lambs girds the apse perimeter. The altar rests on a broad stepped platform, separated from the nave by a communion rail. The altar, built of marble, has inset panels in its face and a square tabernacle behind the top of the altar, with a light-brown marble face with side panels with gold tile banding featuring mosaics with grapes. Flanking the tabernacle are slender towers holding angel statues. Above the altar, a tall marble shrine-like arched open-faced chamber holds a marble crucifix surmounted by an an ornate round panel featuring a molded or carved risen Christ figure with an almost oversized halo, all encircled with a band with a Latin inscription: *"Evis in obitv nro prae sentia mvhamvr."*

The church's interior reveals the ongoing decline of the Gothic style in this second decade of the twentieth century with basic departure from the once-prevailing intersecting vaulted ceiling, here at St. John's, employing an assembly of flat ceiling beams with complex molding, accented by leafy modillions in the ceiling panels. The floor plan is based on the traditional basilica plan of long rectangular nave wall with a series of column-supported arched openings bearing upper level clerestory walls holding its high main ceiling. The main nave is flanked by lower aisle sections, which carry on the Gothic influence with intersecting arched ceilings. Brick piers with inset corners are capped. The outward face of the chamber has flattened engaged columns with a half-round arch above. A half-round brick arch, approximately two feet wide and projecting from the side walls and ceiling, uses alternating courses of orange-yellow and beige-yellow brick with corner edges of sliver-yellow brick. A band of grape bunches with leafy vines painted on the brick run vertically on the brick arch faces.

Stations of the Cross have sculptured figures on gilded pedestals. The nave is lighted by hanging hexagonal lanterns. A brick wainscot lines the nave. A rose stained-glass window has a prominent location above the choir loft.

The remarkable architecture of Saint John the Baptist Catholic Church provides an example of how great architecture occasionally arises, not from adroitly following all of the rules, but from imaginatively stepping in and out of them. Saint John's' unique design stands distinctly, and with aesthetic aplomb, apart but at least equal to the plenitude of excellent churches in Stearns County.

# Melrose
# Church of St. Mary

Architect: George Bergmann, St.Cloud
Builder: E.D. Richmond, Melrose
1898

## Parish History

The city of Melrose, located along I-94 thirty-five miles west of St. Cloud was founded by Yankee-Americans in the late 1850s. These first settlers established farms on land which later became the town of Melrose. The arrival of the St. Paul and Pacific Railroad in 1871 initiated an influx of settlers, first the Irish who took jobs with the railroad, and later Germans who established farms in the area. Melrose quickly became a thriving commercial center.

The first Catholic church in Melrose was established in 1872 and was named St. Patrick's. The nationality of the founders was Irish, and they were initially served by a Benedictine priest from St. John's, Father Augustine Burns. Their congregation continued to grow, numbering 250 by 1884.

Meanwhile, the second wave of immigrants, German Catholics, was beginning, and they soon outnumbered the Irish. Their wish to have religious services in their own language prompted a group to request that a new parish be formed. The bishop honored the request, and in 1878, the church of St. Boniface

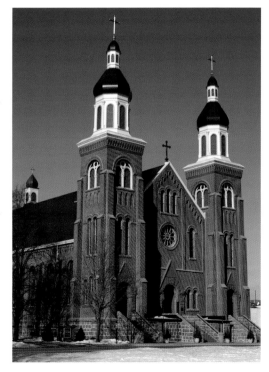

was established. A wood-framed church was built in 1879, and enlarged in 1895, due to the rapid growth of the parish. Under the leadership of their pastor, Monsignor Bernard Richter, plans for an even larger church were soon initiated. Construction began in 1897, and in 1899 the present Romanesque structure was completed. .

St. Patrick's parish suffered a loss of membership in 1922 when the headquarters of the Great Northern Railroad moved to Waite Park, near St. Cloud. Many of the Irish families moved away to find other work, and by the early 1930s, less than 100 families remained. In 1958, the bishop decided that St. Patrick's would be dissolved and that its members would become part of the St. Boniface parish, which he renamed St. Mary's. In order to bring about unity, the much-loved pastor at St. Patrick's, Father Francis Julig, was named the pastor of St. Mary's. Also, the statue of St. Patrick was moved from the old church to a place on the back altar at St. Mary's at an equal level with that of St. Boniface.

## ARCHITECTURAL DESCRIPTION

Saint Boniface is the largest church in rural Stearns County, built in the Romanesque Revival style with several Gothic features. The church's main façade faces east, with a pair of square 130-foot-high corner towers that make transition at the tops to octagonal belfries supporting onion-shaped domes with Coptic crosses. The church was built with red brick, produced in Menominee, Wisconsin, supported on a massive dark-gray granite blocks quarried in the St. Cloud area, forming the foundation. Nave walls are divided into nine bays with tall stained-glass windows buttressed with slanted gray granite caps, which are centered between brick buttresses. The red brick is given contrast with rock-hewn gray granite trim members, with arched brick corbelling at tops of walls.

The interior of Saint Boniface has a central aisle with two side aisles. The nine bay nave is given stately rhythm by a progression of bundled-like wood columns with foliated elaborate capitals. From these columns spring a progression of arches whose half-circular openings use repeating arch-shaped spaces to buttress the intersecting vault work that forms the nave's ceiling. The lofty plaster vaults are painted with a blue slightly more intense than the typical soft pastel-like tones most Gothic churches in this area have, giving a sense of liveliness to the whole interior. The strong axis of the nave leads to the intricately constructed altar, said to have been built in Germany and shipped to this site.

Color also is rendered in other, more subtle ways. Stained glass windows at the nave walls feature a curvilinear intricate geometric background, with each glazed panel having a predominate soft-hued tint, with brighter colors in religious symbols in the window center. From window to window, the green, blue and rose tones alternate, and the soft white plaster on the splayed walls surrounding these windows picks up these subtle colors, giving gentle emphasis by indirect sunlight filtered through window stained glass, all of which adds to the total, almost mesmerizing effect.

# New Munich
# Church of the
# Immaculate Conception

Architect: Anton Dohmen, Milwaukee
Builder: Herman Jeub, Minneapolis
1910

## Parish History

Shortly after Stearns County had been established in 1855, a surveyor working in the area of the present town of New Munich came upon a small lake surrounded by oak trees. He drew it onto his map and called it Lake Maria. He then inserted a town next to the lake which he named Munich am See (German for Munich on the Lake). This town never materialized, but one mile northwest of the lake a settlement did develop, which was called New Munich. The reason that the new

site was chosen was probably because it was along the path of the oxcart trails which were the only means at the time of transporting supplies to this area as well as to fur trading posts in the northwest part of the state.

The first known settler in the area was Henry Hoppe, who came from Freeport, Illinois. He was soon joined by a large number of others, and soon there was a request for a priest to offer mass in their settlement. Father Clement Staub, a Benedictine priest recently arrived from Pennsylvania, visited on an irregular basis and said mass in the homes. The parish was formally organized in 1861 by Father Pius Bayer. In September of the same year, their first church, a log structure measuring twenty-four by thirty feet was built. The area was growing quickly, and New Munich became the mother parish for others in the area including Freeport, Melrose, and Meire Grove.

In 1873, due to the rapid growth of the parish, a frame church measuring thirty-six by 100 feet was built. This church was used until 1911, when the present Romanesque style church was completed. By 1912 the parish had also completed a rectory and a parochial school. The total cost of all the buildings was $100,000, a very sizable amount of money in those days. Immaculate Conception Church is one of four in Stearns County with two steeples. The other three are in Melrose, Lake Henry, and St. Nicholas.

## ARCHITECTURAL DESCRIPTION

The Church of the Immaculate Conception in New Munich presents a façade with a pair of square towers of unequal height, capped with tall spires. Its high pitched roof has raised pediment gables at front and back in which the stone capped masonry wall extends above the roof plane. The intersecting transept plays a somewhat minor role in the church's exterior architectural statement here, compared to typical Stearns County churches.

The modified Romanesque architecture at Immaculate Conception, characterized by half-circular arched window and door openings, instead of pointed arches, displays a transition from the traditional Gothic style. Other Romanesque motifs are corbelled brick cornices, towers with extended brick corners that treat walls between as panels, all contributing an architectural presence of brick solidity, often emblematic of late nineteenth-century Romanesque buildings.

The foundation of the Church of the Immaculate Conception is granite, originally discovered in an outcropping five miles from town, that was blasted and dressed (finished into blocks) by parishioners.

The Romanesque half-round motif characterizes the interior as well. Intersecting roof vaults, so typically used in Gothic Churches, are structured with half-round arches given a sense of solidity. The architectural expression of intersecting vault work is enriched by the pale-green plaster of vault surfaces, emphasized by ochre arch bands tipped with gold accent. These arch structures are supported by round plaster-surfaced columns with stylized Corinthian capitals that become surmounted by wide flaring overhanging coves. The vaulted ceilings in the side aisles have a barely noticeable pinkish hue. Side wall bays follow the Gothic with large stained-glass windows. The stained glass panels are composed of the typical tall pair of arched top glass panels depicting figurative allegorical scenes, with a quatrefoil modified circular panel above with geometrically composed design of symbolic intention.

The apse is half-octagonal, structured with pointed arches with ribbed edges that clearly define the vault forms. The curved panels between the arches feature round headed tall narrow windows. The free-standing white marble altar has a small baldacchino over the tabernacle, flanked on both sides by smaller baldacchino elements. The main altar and two side altars were fabricated in Italy.

The transept walls seem broader in the interior than they appear on the exterior. Their prominent features are large stained-glass windows with half-circular arched heads. A round window encircled with smaller ones stands above three pointed arched stained-glass windows that feature olive-hued robed human figures holding crooked staffs—male figures on the left-hand side, female figures on the right side. Stations of the Cross are supported by sculptured brackets, with carved figures painted in rich polychromes.

Of special interest is the four-dialed clock in one of the towers, originally donated for the old church and re-installed here, that displays the time and calls out bell tones at the cardinal intervals of the day. The clock's simple mechanical parts, operated by weights that are adjusted daily, has run continuously with little repair for over 100 years.

The Church of the Immaculate Conception in New Munich is a remarkable representation of Gothic integrated with Romanesque, presenting a somewhat monochromatic brick exterior seeming to serve as a vessel for the pleasant interior interplay of structure and embellishment.

## OPOLE
# Church of Our Lady of Mount Carmel
Architect: Charles Hausler, St. Paul
Builder: Dombrouski Brothers, Springfield
1929

### PARISH HISTORY

The tiny hamlet of Opole was founded by immigrants from Poland who came to the United States to escape political and religious oppression in their homeland. The first settlers attended church in North Prairie, a few miles away in Morrison County where the majority of the members were German. Within a short time, the Poles petitioned the bishop to have their own church where sermons could be given in their native language. The bishop was sensitive to their request and sent Polish priests to say mass in the homes of the settlers.

By 1877 over fifty families had arrived in the area and a wood-framed church seating 200 was completed. Services were infrequent until 1891 when Father Kitowski became the first resident pastor. Over the next twenty years, the parish

grew to 130 families. Numbers decreased somewhat in 1910 when a new Polish church in nearby Holdingford was built.

The present church was built during the pastorate of Father Anthony Lamusga. In December of 1928 the trustees approved the design, and Father Lamusga set out on horseback around the parish to raise funds. Construction began the following spring with the excavation done by a group of parishioners using teams of horses and scrapers. The cornerstone was laid on July 28, 1929, with Bishop Joseph Busch officiating. Construction was halted midway when the contractor went bankrupt. Luckily, the parish had requested that a bond be carried by the contractor, so building was resumed by the bonding company. The new church, with a total cost of $50,000, was completed in time for Christmas services.

Most of the money for the church had been raised previous to the start of construction, but the parish still had a debt of several thousand dollars. Father Lamusga urged the parishioners to pay the remaining debt so the church could be consecrated, and within three years this was accomplished despite the onset of the Great Depression, which gripped the nation at the time. An entry written by Father Lamusga in the parish records indicated that after the final payment on the loan was made, only thirteen cents remained in the parish accounts.

## ARCHITECTURAL DESCRIPTION

The exterior of Our Lady of Mount Carmel was designed in the Colonial Revival style by St. Paul architect Charles Hausler, known at that time for several notable churches in that city. The Colonial Revival style, uncommon in Stearns County at that time, had become a prevailing architectural mode across the nation. At Mount Carmel, architectural details were simplified from traditional Gothic while keeping a tall steeple set above a square bell tower. Typical American-built Colonial Revival churches were usually executed in white painted wood siding, but here as elsewhere in Stearns County, brick was the chosen material. The textured dark-red brick is accented with limestone trim.

For the most part, the Colonial Revival exterior architecture indicates the early Polish parish's desire to fit in with the prevalent culture, and much of the interior fulfills the same objective. The exceptions are the stained-glass windows donated by parish members featuring Polish names, and an eastern orthodox stylized painting of the black Madonna is mounted on a nave wall near the sanctuary.

In the interior, Hausler continued the sense of simplicity with subtle handling of basic elements. The half-rounded apse casts focus on the richly ornamented altar with its domed baldachin supported by four diminutive marble columns. Above the tabernacle is a statue of Our Lady of Mount Carmel. The nave walls feature stained arched glass windows hooded with smooth plaster tops splaying inward into the outer edges of the barrel-vaulted nave ceiling. The effect Hausler created with regularly reoccurring elements in their passage through the nave is a pleasant subtle interior expression.

In the context of architectural style progression in Stearns County, this church in Opole becomes an evident shift from the complexity of Gothic's overt ribbed demarcations and profuse decorative features toward simpler architectural expression, characterized by plasticity of continuous molded form. Hausler accomplished this effort while skillfully concentrating orna-mental features that become items of visual interest unto themselves, not as duty for embellishments of structure. This design method presaged an early step in the emergence of modernism, as Our Lady of Mount Carmel offers a lesson in integrating smooth shaping of form with the appropriate prescription of ornament, later discarded by architectural Modernism.

# RICHMOND
# Church of Sts. Peter and Paul

Architect and Builder: Unknown
1884

## PARISH HISTORY

In 1855, the same year that Stearns County was formed, a group of German settlers arrived in the area of Richmond by oxcart by way of Coal County,

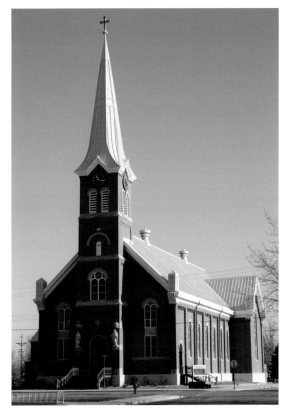

Missouri, and made claim to land near Thyen's lake. The following year, 1856, was a pivotal one in the history of the parish. In that year, Father Pierz visited the area and said mass and urged the settlers to build a church. A sixteen-by-twenty-foot log structure was completed the same year. The Benedictine priests arrived in the area at the same time, and Father Bruno Riess was assigned the care of the parish.

This good fortune was short-lived however when on August 15, following a mission conducted at the church, a grasshopper invasion devastated the area devouring the crops which were nearing harvest. Despite this setback, the area continued to grow at a rapid rate, and, in 1860, a larger frame church was completed. In 1864, St. Peter and Paul's was assigned its

first resident pastor, Father Cornelius Wittmann. A third and larger church was completed in 1866 to accommodate the ever increasing congregation.

The present church was started in 1884 and dedicated in September of 1885. Continual improvements were made to the church over the years including a complete decoration of the walls and ceiling in 1931 by German artist Berthold Von Imhoff. His oil paintings on the ceiling panels depict saints considered to be holy helpers. Devotions to these saints are made in times of sickness and trouble. According to the norms of Vatican II, changes were made to the interior of the church, including removal of the side altars and constructing an altar facing the congregation.

## ARCHITECTURAL DESCRIPTION

Saint Peter and Paul's Church gives an arresting architectural dominance to the large space it occupies near the middle of this apparently thriving agricultural community. As with so many German Catholic Gothic churches, Saint Peter and Paul's closely follows the German Gothic prototype of a slightly projecting single tower centered on the façade. Its red-brick walls are a subtle display of simple pilasters that frame round, arched stained glass windows, and brick corbelling at the top of the walls lend a sense of support to the roof edges immediately above. Two interesting features of this Gothic-influenced structure give it a modest individuality: its metal clad roof and its steeple's curved, flared corner edges that work in nice proportion with small angled gable shapes centered on each face of the tower.

The church interior however, departs from the German Gothic norm, as Saints Peter and Paul seems intent to present an expansive space, unbroken by rows of columns and intersecting curved roof vaults common in typical country church architecture in Stearns County. Also unlike its German Gothic counterparts, Saint Peter and Paul's interior surfaces are defined much more by painted flat surface decorative patterns than by the three dimensionality of architectural elements such as moldings, articulated column capitals, and statuary. The major interior feature is the series of framed oil paintings depicting Stations

SAINT CATHARINE

of the Cross. The nave ceiling is constructed as a five-part series of flat-sur-faced panels running front to back. Those panels are subdivided into rectan-gular panels by thin almost imperceptible ribs edged by dark-brown painted bands that visually define the panels. Elaborate painted tracery lends a two-dimensional articulation to the ceiling and walls as well.

The main nave space widens slightly in the form of a shallow transept. A large arched opening leads to the sanctuary, narrower in width than the nave. Within the sanctuary is a free-standing altar assembly, composed of a relatively small altar with a three-part backing structure. Its well-proportioned structure has arched openings surmounted by flat-topped entablatures, all embellished with classical Renaissance-inspired details. The design is more representative of Romanesque architecture, in subtle contrast to Saint Peter and Paul's Gothic exterior.

# Rockville
# Church of Mary of the Immaculate Conception

Architect: Father Raphael Knapp, Collegeville
Builder: Henry Steckling, St. Cloud
1911

## Parish History

In most of Stearns County, the formation of a parish and the construction of the first church closely followed the initial settlement of an area. In Rockville, it was fifty years between the first settlement and the building of the church. The reason for this delay was largely due to the proximity of several other parishes including those in Cold Spring, Luxemburg, and St. Nicholas.

The first settlers around Rockville were of English and Scottish descent and built businesses in the town along the Sauk River. Later settlement by mainly German farmers claimed the available land in the area suitable for farming. The granite industry quickly became the biggest employer in the area, and by the turn of the century, Rockville became a thriving town. Its quarries supplied the granite for the Cathedral of St. Paul, built between 1906 and 1914.

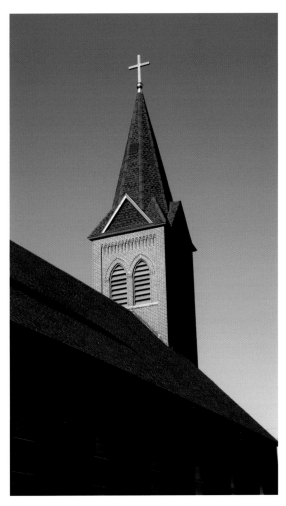

By 1911, Catholics in the area started a petition to form their own parish. With permission granted, the parish was quickly incorporated, and the first order of business was to build a church. This project had the cooperation of the whole town, Catholics and non-Catholics alike. The owners of the local quarries donated the granite for the foundations, while the employees cut the stone. Bricks were hauled from the railroad station to the church site by the youth of the community. The first mass was celebrated in the completed church on December 8, 1911, the Feast of the Immaculate Conception. Less than six months had passed between the incorporation of the parish and the completion of the church.

The loans secured to build the church were paid off in 1917, and during the next several years, the interior furnishings, including the altars and stained glass windows were completed, most donated by parishioners.

## ARCHITECTURAL DESCRIPTION

The Church of Mary of the Immaculate Conception is immediately visible along the main street in the hamlet of Rockville. Its tall spire rising above the centrally-positioned bell tower slightly projects from its façade. The church's Gothic features give it an architectural propriety, which makes this red-brick church the most aesthetically rewarding structure in its immediate community and the region around it.

Gothic pointed arched windows in the bell tower and along nave walls, the steep roof with corbelled edges at the façade, and the pointed arch main doorway opening give the façade simplicity that is well tempered in composition. Brick corbelling details refine that composition, as they appear in the façade along the sloping roof edge, define measured levels at various heights in the bell tower, and give a defined upper edge to the nave walls.

The architectural simplicity continues in the interior. Immediately apparent is the three-part vaulted ceiling in the nave, what might be assumed to be supported by a hammer-beam roof structure, in which central arches are supported on each end by lesser half-arches that are supported from upper nave walls. This unusual ceiling vaulting appears in a few other Stearns churches, with vault surfaces typically covered with plaster, tin-plate panels, or fiberboard sheets. In this interior, deep-toned knotty pine with beaded edges line the ceiling vaulting, with wood-faced arches, apparently applied to the actual structure above ceiling surfaces, running approximately twelve feet apart, in transverse fashion across the width of the space.

The wall separating the nave from the sanctuary has a slightly pointed arched opening with blind (recessed into the wall without opening through) arched forms on each side. Within the sanctuary, the five-sided apse walls are clad with partial-height wood paneling on the side and angled wall faces, with the plaster-covered center wall holding a small crucifix. The altar area shows evidence of being significantly revised by Vatican II reforms, as the granite altar table at the outer edge of the sanctuary and a similar shaped table holding the bronze square tabernacle are the principal architectural elements that define this space.

ROSCOE

# Church of St. Agnes

Architect: Charles Hausler, St Paul
Builder: Dombrouski Brothers, Springfield
1929

## PARISH HISTORY

In 1886 the Great Northern Railroad built a line through Roscoe, and trains made regular stops there, as it was the halfway point between St. Cloud and Willmar. Soon many businesses sprang up around the depot, and talk started about building a church. Early settlers in the area had been attending mass in nearby parishes in St. Martin and Richmond. The plans developed by the settlers were ambitious and included both a church and a rectory on land which was donated by Gregor Kost. With permission from the bishop granted, plans were drawn by St. Cloud architect George Bergmann for a wood-framed structure that was forty by one hundred feet. The completed church was dedicated by Bishop Trobec in October of 1898 and was named St. Agnes, the name of the parish the

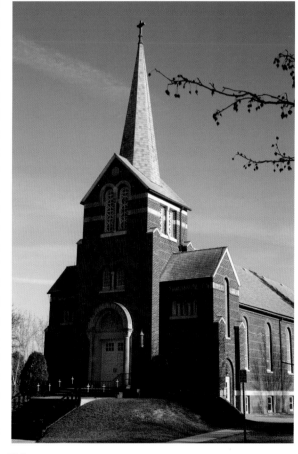

bishop had previously served in St. Paul. Interior finishing proceeded over the next ten years.

On September 4, 1928, soon after extensive remodeling and redecorating of the interior had been completed, the church burned to the ground. No time was wasted in the planning for the new church. Records show that the foundations for the new structure were completed in November, just two months after the fire, and the new church was completed in the fall of 1929.

## ARCHITECTURAL DESCRIPTION

The facade of the church of Saint Agnes displays a grafting of the Colonial Revival Style to the Gothic Revival-Romanesque hybrid. The centered square tall bell tower, topped with a pointed spire projecting from a gabled nave roof continues the Gothic's progression throughout all corners of Stearns County. However, the second decade of the twentieth century signals Gothic-Romanesque being absorbed by emerging styles such as the Colonial Revival, in evidence here at Saint Agnes. The vestibule section, narrow by its function, set slightly back from the bell tower, distinguishes itself from the nave by its gabled roof running across the facade rather than the vestibule's typical integration within the front nave structure, as the Gothic style insists on doing. Colonial Revival appears above the façade's entrance doors with an arched band with highly articulated broad leaf alternating patterns, serving to frame the inset half-round tympanum with its sculptured relief of Saint Agnes holding a lamb and by winged angel heads.

Saint Agnes was designed by architect Charles Hausler, whose St. Paul professional practice contributed introduction of style elements common in non-ecclesiastical buildings that fit Stearns County's Gothic design standards.

Other Colonial Revival features are the reduced arched windows with multiple panes set in muntins (thin wood cross-connected members) instead of stained glass held in leaded strips, paired at the bell tower shaft and in triple sets at the vestibule walls. Also, the transition from square bell tower to its spire is more abrupt, although made graceful, but unlike the staged stepping back of the square shaft and mini-corner spires that Gothic architects loved to fuss with. The reduced height of the nave walls of this smaller-scaled church bring the roof closer to the main floor, resulting in absence of clerestory windows that higher walls are able to provide.

Saint Agnes's interior floor layout has a main center aisle with narrow side aisles, nave walls with four round top stained-glass windows at each side wall. An ornamented rope-shaped molding runs across the top of both side walls of the nave. The modified barrel vault ceiling of Romanesque influence features transverse ribs, giving support where they reach the walls by florid shaped gold-painted haunches.

The altar area shows signs of the effects of Vatican II's intent to distill the architectural articles of faith by removing ornament and simplifying detail in favor of modernism. What likely was an elaborate altar backpiece is gone; the altar itself transformed into a table with a conspicuous sense of the ordinary, with side altars removed, and the arched opening filled with paneling.

What becomes apparent with this church, smaller in comparison to churches in larger towns of the county, is that it reflects the ability of this much less populated community to build a house of worship of a smaller size in terms of floor area and height, and a modest degree of ornament, enough to express the community's sense of faith. A more intimate architectural scale works here without the grandeur of larger edifices.

# St. Anna
# Church of the Immaculate Conception

Architect: Unknown
Builders:Joseph Marsolek, masonry
Joseph Schellinger and Frank Dobis, woodwork
1902

## Parish History

This church at St. Anna is situated in one of the most picturesque areas of Stearns County, overlooking Pelican Lake and surrounded by rolling hills. The Polish settlers, who arrived here in the 1870s and 1880s, initially attended church in nearby Avon, but soon became interested in building their own church where religious services could be given in their native language. In 1887 a group led by Paul Hennek approached Bishop Seidenbusch and asked for permission to establish a parish on land Hennek donated. The bishop was sympathetic to their cause, and the settlers started immediately on the construction of a wood-frame church, which was dedicated later that year. Initially, Father Peter Chowaniec, pastor at Sobieski in Morrison County, served the parish by offering mass on a monthly basis. Later, the young parish was served by priests

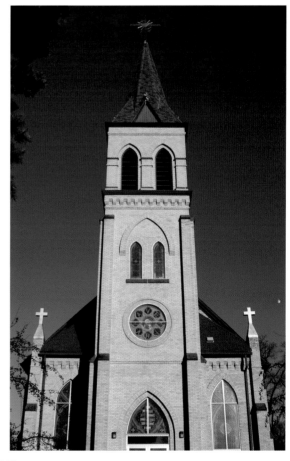

from St. John's Abbey as well as the pastor at St. Mary's in Holdingford. In 1896 Father Anthony Kitowski became the first resident pastor at St. Anna. From the thirty families who comprised the parish in 1887, the congregation had grown to eighty-five families by 1898.

Tragedy struck on June 28, 1902, when the church burned to the ground. Plans were made to rebuild, and in the same year construction on the present church began. The men of the parish donated much of the labor including excavation of the basement, and later hauling the brick from the brickyard in Little Falls. An article in the *St. Cloud Times* relates that during the construction of the present church several workers were preparing to leave for the day and noticed a few men still working high up in the steeple. They quietly removed the ladders from the steeple and left for the day. When they returned the following morning expecting to find the stranded men in the steeple, they found nobody. Evidently the men had lowered themselves to the ground by the ropes they normally used to hoist materials up the steeple.

The completed church was dedicated in October of 1903. By this time, the parish had grown to 100 families with a total of 690 people. In 1911 these numbers decreased when about forty of the families left to join St. Hedwig's parish, which had been established in nearby Holdingford.

Immaculate Conception church was placed on the National Register of Historic Places in 1982

## ARCHITECTURAL DESCRIPTION

Saint Anna's beige-yellow brick walls and steep roof with a pointed steeple presents the simple rectitude of the Gothic adaptation that is common to Stearns County. Foremost at the façade is a prominent square bell tower rising straight up from the main entrance, following the architectural rules of three parts: the shaft rising from the main entrance two-thirds of its height, a slightly set-in bell chamber with pair of louvered pointed arch openings, then its top with its square base tapering to an eight-sided steeple. The corners of the bell tower have somewhat diminutive pilasters that step back as they flow up the shaft, and the pilaster motif appears in regular intervals along the walls of the nave.

The interior nave of Immaculate Conception is likewise obedient to Gothic principles. Similar to many church structures in this region's rural hamlets, exterior walls extend straight up, without an upper section of clerestory windows set in walls supported on series of columns. This means ceiling vaults span uninterrupted from wall to wall over the relatively narrow floor plate. Those vaults form sharp-edged curved surfaces that spring from knob-shaped projecting brackets engaged on nave walls, reaching across the main longitudinal main ceiling vault.

Unusually wide stained glass windows with pointed arched tops continue the Gothic theme. Immaculate Conception's altar, crafted in rich and intricate detail, varnished and gold-tipped, stands before an even more finely detailed reredos.

Very similar to other Gothic churches in Stearns County, this reredos serves the church's architecture principal duty—to draw the eyes of worshippers' to devotion.

## St. Anthony
# Church of St. Anthony
Architect and builder: unknown
1897

### Parish History

When Father Pierz visited his homeland of Carniola in 1864, he convinced many of his countrymen to immigrate to Stearns County. A good number settled in St. Stephen, making it the first Slovenian settlement in the United States. Another group pushed further west, establishing farms around the present town of St. Anthony. In fact, the township is called Krain Township for the province in Slovenia where they had originated, and St. Anthony was, for a time called Kraintown.

Anton Gogola was among the first to arrive, and the first masses in the area were conducted in his home in 1867. By 1870 Father Joseph Buh, a Slovenian priest offered mass at two-week intervals. The early settlers were soon joined by German and Dutch families, increasing the size of the parish considerably. In 1872 work was underway on their first church, made from logs and measuring thirty by fifty feet. Construction on the present church was started in 1897 and completed in 1901. In the years that followed, the interior was furnished and stained-glass windows were installed.

### Architectural Description

The Church of Saint Anthony's tall steeple becomes a landmark rising above the horizontal expanses of surrounding farm fields. Viewing the church close up, the central bell tower's corner pilasters project outward at a diagonal angle from the square base and step back in vertical sequences toward the upper reaches where the square shape makes transition to an octagonal shape from which the spire points up into the sky. In this manner, Saint Anthony contributes to the classic iconography of rural Gothic brick churches. The bell tower's distinguishing feature is a detail—the transition from the tower's square masonry base to its wood-clad octagonal shaft are dark-brown stone caps with shallow flat tops stepping back, each step widening as they rise, reaching a top stone band girding the bottom face of the octagonal upper tower.

Beige brick, fabricated from a clay native to the St. Cloud area, form the church's walls. The façade walls, sloped to follow the roof, are capped with dark-brown stone giving a nice contrast to the brick, and a series of elongated corbels contribute to the simple elegance of Saint Anthony.

Saint Anthony's interior is similar to many smaller Stearns County churches, with medium-height nave walls uninterrupted by colonnades dividing side aisles, and without a transept. The ceiling is unusual—a stepped type of barrel vault rises at the top of each nave wall, curving into a quarter circle shape, then surmounted by center half-circle vault. The ceiling is clad with a type of fiberboard rectangular panels, probably covering the original ceiling material.

The altar area exhibits an array of intricate wood details astutely designed to reinforce a proportional monumentality. In warm-toned varnished wood accented gold and blue, this tripartite assemblage serves to express the symbolic tenets of the Catholic faith.

At first glance, these Catholic churches in Stearns County and nearby areas built by Eastern European and Polish communities seem to adhere to a Gothic-Romanesque architecture established by German immigrants. But ethnic identity here at Saint Anthony is on display in this altar area, with an icon-like painting of the Madonna prominently set above the center of the altar.

# St. Augusta
# Church of St. Mary
# Help of Christians

Architect: Fr.Gregory Steil
Builder: Unknown
1873

## Parish History

In the early 1850s, German immigrants arrived in the area by steamboat, and soon a small settlement developed along the Mississippi, just south of St. Cloud. By 1854 a townsite was platted consisting of 250 acres on land owned by John Wilson of St. Cloud. Father Pierz was the first priest to visit the settlers and offer mass for them. On one of his trips to the area, he found a prayer card on the ground with a picture of St. Augustine on it and suggested that a church be built at this location. This log structure was completed in 1856 and the settlement was named St. Augusta. Over the next several years, Benedictine priests visited the mission to offer mass and the sacraments.

A second larger frame church was erected in 1858. Father Valentine Stimmler took charge of the parish in 1872, becoming the first resident pastor at St. Augusta. The area continued to grow, and during a mission by

Father Wenninger in 1873, a cross was erected at a location one mile west of the original townsite. It was at this site that the present church was built.

The new church was forty-eight by 132 feet and constructed of locally quarried granite hauled to the site by the parishioners. As the walls were constructed, scaffolds were erected with ramps, and the granite blocks were put in

carts and pushed up the ramps to the level where they were needed. The completed structure was dedicated in 1875. With few modifications, it continues to serve the parish at the present time. The mission cross from 1873 has been faithfully restored and stands near the entrance to the church. In 1982 the church was placed on the National Register of Historic Places.

## ARCHITECTURAL DESCRIPTION

The Gothic-styled Saint Mary Help of Christians is one of several moderately sized stone churches in Stearns County. These edifices tend to share several architectural characteristics, such as nave walls running straight without clerestories from ground to roof edge, random coursing of granite stone, unornamented exterior surfaces, and square bell tower shafts centered on the façade and rising unbroken without step-backs and capped by slender steeples. Saint Mary's is also one of several Catholic churches in the area that has built new additions located on the front and sides of the

traditional church façade. Although historic preservationists tend to think these additions despoil the historic integrity of these churches, they become more acceptable if the new architecture is done right. Such is the case with Saint Mary's. A studied observation indicates the massive stone verticality finds architectural companionship, mostly by way of sensitive contrast. The original structure's stone imparts a heavy and muscular aspect that sets against the addition's demure lightly-framed modernity, with its large glass expanses and low sloped simple roof forms that provide neutral background.

In the interior, the nave's clear-span barrel-vault ceiling above a wide center aisle forms a definite axis from the vestibule to the sanctuary without the rigidity of many axis-oriented churches. Having no transept that gives a section of extra width to the nave, the eye is given uninterrupted travel toward the sanctuary, where the altar and its elaborate reredos rewards one's visual appetite. An intricately staged series of columns and arches built with richly

varnished hardwood, festooned with gold-tipped embellishments giving articulated edges to copious architectural detail. In a few words—the altar and
backdrop serve Saint Mary's parishioners with a rich visual treat.

Up within the reredos and away from the altar area, the statuary within the sanctuary is a study in itself. The central open-faced chamber recessed
in the woodwork shelters a crucifix, with slightly smaller flanking chambers
holding Mary and Joseph, all bordered at the corners with angels in their cus-
tomary obligation of bowing in reverence to the three figures. The side altars
just outside the sanctuary feature statues of saints in front of similarly elaborate backdrops. Stained glass windows with intricate patterns are encased in
deep window openings along nave walls.

Saint Mary Help of Christians offers a wealth of ecclesiastical architecture within its modest 1870s-era granite shell, reflecting the high aspirations of the church's early immigrant community that were met with architectural success.

## St. Augusta
# St. Boniface Chapel
### 1877-1961

This tiny chapel is located on a hilly and wooded site, halfway between the parish churches in St. Augusta and Luxemburg. Like the original Grasshopper Chapel in Cold Spring, it was built by the adjacent parishes in response to the

grasshopper plague which had devastated the crops during the summers of 1876 and 1877. It was named for St. Boniface, the patron saint of the German people. The first procession to the chapel took place shortly after its completion. In the following years, the pilgrimages were made every year on June 5, the feast day of St. Boniface. By the late 1880s interest in continuing the tradition had waned, and the chapel fell into disrepair. For a time it was used as a tool shed by the owner of the farm on which it was located.

In 1961 a story in a local publication about area chapels renewed interest in preserving St. Boniface Chapel. Volunteers from the parishes in St. Augusta and Luxemburg carefully restored the structure using as much of its original material as they could. Masses are held there annually to pray for good crops.

Rebuilt to its original form after decades in disrepair, Saint Boniface Chapel measures twelve feet wide by fifteen and a half feet in length, built of materials typical to garage construction. The structure has a simple gable roof, two double-hung windows with arched heads on each side, and a pair of hinged doors made from tongue and groove wood paneling. Narrow lap wood siding with corner board trim is painted white.

The interior contains an eight-foot-high flat ceiling and the floor has a raised altar platform supporting a small wood altar, built with cabinet construction, painted white with gold paint edging on the door panels. On the left side of the altar, a statue of Saint Boniface is mounted on a wall-hung bracket, and on the right side, a statue of Joseph is similarly positioned. The chapel appears to be unheated and without electricity or plumbing.

## St. Cloud

# Church of St. John Cantius

Architect: Unknown
Builders: Joseph Marsolek, masonry
Joseph Schellinger, woodwork
1901

### Parish History

Most of the Polish immigrants who settled in Stearns County in the 1870s and 1880s were farmers and established parishes in Opole, Holdingford, and St. Anna. However many came to the area to work in the growing granite and railroad companies, and these Poles settled in St. Cloud. Starting their own parish and building a church was difficult, so they attended nearby St. Mary's, a German-speaking parish. By 1886 a Polish speaking priest, Father John Sroka from Gilman in Benton County, was given charge of the Poles in St. Cloud. Mass was offered in the basement of Holy Angels church for a number of years.

In 1893 Bishop Zardetti gave permission to start a Polish National parish, and encouraged a fundraising campaign to build a church. The money wasn't raised quickly, but the donation of land by several parishioners moved the process of building a church closer to reality. On March 7, 1896, the parish was incorporated and plans began for building a church. Actual construction began in the spring of 1901 and the finished church was dedicated on December 27 of the same year. Much of the labor was donated, and financial help was received from St. Cloud businesses. The parishioners pledged money as well. The church was named for St. John Cantius a fifteenth-century priest known for his generosity to the poor.

## ARCHITECTURAL DESCRIPTION

Saint John Cantius, located in a residential neighborhood in Saint Cloud, occupies a corner lot in the most urban setting of all the fifty-two Catholic churches in Stearns County. Its architectural form is a straightforward rectangular gable-roofed red-brick structure in the Romanesque Revival style. Saint John Cantius is similar to other Stearns County Catholic churches built in this period, with its bell tower's central position on the façade in the tradition of the Gothic style. Atop the bell tower, set in from the top of its masonry wall, is a dome structure clad in copper details, that supports a much narrower elevated dome-shaped pinnacle feature often used in Polish church architecture. This church is in keeping with so many other places of worship in the county whose modest size maintains architectural order by careful proportion of its design features, requiring the architect to be no less skilful than what is needed for more monumental edifices. Also similar to several of these rural churches, the narrow floor plan uses clear-span roof framing over the nave instead of a high main roof supported by rows of columns between the central seating area and the lower roofed seating areas on each side.

Architectural propriety is in place in the interior of Saint John's. The nave's clear-span vaulted ceiling is a simple form, but ever so finely articulated with decorative pressed-tin panels as a surface material. Round arched stained glass windows give rich illuminated colored light to the interior.

## St. Cloud

# St. Mary's Cathedral

Architect: Nairne Fisher, St. Cloud
Builder: Edward Hirt and Sons, St. Cloud, lower level
A.G. Wahl and Sons, St. Cloud, superstructure
1921- 1930

### Parish History

The Saint Mary's parish has the dual distinction of being the mother church of the city of St. Cloud as well as the seat of the Diocese of St. Cloud.

Father Pierz, who had arrived in the area in 1852 and said mass in the homes of the earliest settlers in St. Cloud, purchased land where the present

church sits in 1855 from John Wilson, often referred to as the father of St. Cloud. The first church, measuring twenty-five by thirty-five feet was built in 1856 and was called the church of Saint Mary of the Immaculate Conception. With the influx of Catholics to St. Cloud, a larger church was needed, and in 1861, the first resident pastor, Father Clement Staub, began to make plans. His successor continued the process, and by 1865 this church, done in the Gothic style had been completed. It was an impressive building measuring one hundred forty-five by sixty-four feet and seating over six hundred people.

On August 25, 1920, the church was destroyed by fire, and plans were started immediately for a new and larger church. Father Luke Fink, pastor at the time of the fire, contacted John Comes, a Pittsburgh architect, who drew the plans for the foundation and a basement church. This structure was completed in 1921 and served the parish for ten years.

During this time, architects were secured for the superstructure. Nairne Fisher, who had moved from New York to partner with St. Cloud architect Leo Schaefer, was selected. The brick Romanesque basilica-style church was blessed on April 26, 1931. In 1933 a fire destroyed Holy Angel's church which had served as the pro-Cathedral for the Diocese. However it wasn't until 1937 that Saint Mary's was named the Cathedral for the Diocese of St. Cloud.

## ARCHITECTURAL DESCRIPTION

The Cathedral of the St. Cloud Diocese occupies a site at the edge of St. Cloud's downtown district, where its tall brick campanile makes its urban location recognizable. Saint Mary's architecture was modeled after a sixth-century Byzantine basilica-style church, Sant'Appollinare, in Ravenna, Italy. Its construction commenced in 1921, with its first phase being a basement finished for services until the main structure was completed in 1931.

The exterior form of Saint Mary's follows the Byzantine mode in a manner that breaks from the once-omnipresent but now depleted Gothic/Romanesque nineteenth-century form. This revival of the Byzantine architectural form with origins five centuries before the advent of Gothic adventurism delineates how the evolution of architecture occasionally looks backward in a pause before the next movement develops. The long basilica plan gains more longitudinal emphasis by its sheer length of the nave. Saint Mary's upper nave section features a moderately sloped clay-tile roof, flanked by wide side-aisle roofed structures that cross over the façade to form a portico with a central colonnade that shelters the main entrance. The columns are made of local granite given a smooth surface and give a clue to the architectural origins with Byzantine-influenced capitals. The campanile bell tower stands independently from the main body of the church at its rear left side, its slender square form displays perforated stone inset panels in the upper portion of the shaft and a low-sloped hip roof.

The massing of the exterior is a composition of simple forms; the flat brick-wall surfaces have no offset and inset panels, and are broken only by minor corbelling bands under roof eaves and slightly projecting brick bands that frame the cathedral's modest-sized window openings.

Throughout the spectrum of noteworthy architecture, simple forms often receive enrichment from subtlety, and the Cathedral of Saint Mary provides a

fine example. Several flat wall planes contain bands of brickwork with geometric patterns and stacked soldier courses, augmented by the generous use of richer colors within the range of brick medium brown and soft orange tones.

Saint Mary's nave has a strong longitudinal orientation, along with its high ceiling, lending a narrow aspect to the space. But the overall architectural character is one of design finesse. The architect's employment of the basilica style establishes colonnades supporting the two parallel nave upper walls. In typical basilica fashion, these colonnades divide the main nave's high and moderately sunlit space from the side aisles, whose lower ceilings and narrow slit-like windows form softly darker spaces. The result is an architectural expression created here by simple use of differing qualities of light.

But the structure's design sense gathers its strength, again with simplicity, in exercises of subtlety; the series of arched openings supported by the colonnades are framed with slightly projecting semicircular plaster bands in the same color as the nave walls. Above, thin pilasters rise softly above the columns, forming barely perceptible vertical frames to give centering to pairs of diminutively sized windows set high in the clerestory walls. Although these windows appear to be much smaller than clerestory windows of Gothic churches that typically offer architectural competition to the lofty vault-work, this design application allows these upper walls to reinforce the horizontality that drives the structure's design. Moreover, opposite of the Gothic example, the smaller windows appear properly subservient to the geometry of the beams that support the flat ceiling, made up with major transverse beams that provide architectural counter-play to the nave's longitudinal axis and the minor purlin members that obey it.

A large semicircular archway provides transition to the sanctuary beyond—a transition of both architectural space and Catholic mid-twentieth-century institutional change. Whereas the nave hews to the centuries-old basilica form, the sanctuary is outfitted with tradition-breaking Vatican II interior design. Here at the Cathedral of Saint Mary, the architectural minimalism ushered in by Vatican II has gained a respectful accommodation with

original architecture. All vestiges of the original altar and surrounding appur-
tenances are gone, replaced with modernist minimalist layered and stepped
geometry, rendered in monochromatic gray granite. Whereas the granite of the
columns with the nave feature marbleized swirls and a highly polished surface, Vatican II granite in the sanctuary has a matte texture. The altar now facing the parishioners has an uncomplicated design to express the table aspect
of its function. Behind, a simple upright granite slab supplies a visual blank
background to define the religious event around the altar. A counterpoint to
the rectangularity of the solid granite geometry is the slender and graceful
exposed organ pipework, in front of the apse, artfully arranged in sets that
flank the cable-suspended crucifix. The pipework's round silvery cylinders of
varying heights that create uplifting musical tones seem to serve a time-hon-
ored duty, like the bowing and genuflecting angels facing the cross in the
churches of the centuries.

ST. JOSEPH

# Church of St. Joseph

Architects: Leonard and Sheire, St. Paul
1870–1884

## PARISH HISTORY

When approaching St. Joseph from the west, the Gothic spire of St. Joseph's Church and the dome of the Sacred Heart Chapel at the College of St. Benedict give a European aspect to the town. St. Joseph's is the oldest Catholic church still in use in Stearns County and the oldest consecrated church in the state of Minnesota.

The first German settler in the area was Peter Loso, born in the Rhineland region of Germany, who arrived in 1854 from Indiana. He was soon joined several other families who made up the nucleus of the settlement, originally called Clinton. Father Pierz made his first visit in the fall of 1854 to say mass, and returned in February of 1855 when he urged the settlers to build a church. A twenty-by-thirty log structure was completed in 1856. At the same time, the first Benedictine priests came to the area from

Latrobe Pennsylvania, and provided religious services on a more regular basis. The area grew at a rapid pace, numbering 180 families by 1869.

As early as 1867 plans were being made for a larger church, and with the arrival of Father Cornelius Wittmann as pastor in 1868, these plans became more concrete. An architect was hired to design the church, and over the winter of 1869-1870, fieldstones from the surrounding area were being hauled in for the foundation. Actual construction began in the spring of 1870. The cornerstone was laid on June 5 of the same year and the church was consecrated in June of 1871. It was constructed of fieldstone and split-faced granite, both of which were plentiful in the area, and the parishioners provided most of the labor.

The adjacent rectory, built in the same style as the church and with the same materials, was finished in 1874. The steeple was added in 1884 when enough money had been raised.

## ARCHITECTURAL DESCRIPTION

As the oldest church in Stearns County, the architecture of Saint Joseph offers the simplicity commanded by stone that creates its Gothic form. Flat-

face hewn granite stones in a range of colors of charcoal-gray laid in random order with contrasting light-gray mortar joints compose the walls. The façade's architectural composition consists of a square bell tower projecting from the wall plane, with four slender stepped stone pilasters at the bell tower corners and similar-scaled pilasters that frame the corners of the façade wall.

A steep-pitched roof covers the nave in typical Gothic style; unusually narrow stained glass windows lend to the sense of massiveness of the stone walls, which are given basic articulation by stone buttresses set between the windows. The Gothic influence is readily identifiable with the steep spire rising above miniature spires capping corner pilasters, pointed arched windows and the overall verticality in the proportions of architectural elements, but does not depend on ornamented detail. In this respect, the architecture of the exterior presages what was later to occur in the interior.

The church itself is the major component of a building complex, with a low link that connects the church's east side to a parish house—all constructed in stone and sharing similar architectural features and all making a handsome composition.

The interior of Saint Joseph immediately reveals, if not declares, its mid-twentieth century extreme makeover from traditional Gothic to Vatican II. Here embellishment by detail became replaced by minimalist rectangularity forsaking detail.

In almost all Stearns County Catholic churches, what can be termed the Vatican II effect, the changes to adhere to the new doctrine have been much more liturgical that architectural. In particular, the celebration of services has been relocated to a simple table-altar in the front part of the sanctuary permitting the priest and attending celebrants to face the faithful, and the communion railing became frequently removed to both physically and symbolically place priest and parishioners in a physical setting of communion. Meanwhile, the strong sense of tradition—the overt ornamentalism of the altar, its fanciful back-structure and all the surrounding articulated surfaces —remained firmly in place, the net result amounting to tradition finessing Vatican II.

Saint Joseph however, is thoroughly modern and completely Vatican II, at least from below the arched ceiling vaults. Immediately below where those arches rest on supporting columns, those vertical members are square plain-faced and oak clad with transparent varnish. Nave walls are pure white, planar expanses, dramatically accented with narrow-window splayed openings chiseled into deep recesses.

The altar area, as in traditional churches, functions as the principal focus of the place of worship, and the word "functional" is most operative here. Vatican II employed the architectural modernism mode, whose cardinal dictum, "form follows function," is readily apparent at Saint Joseph. The 1971 renovation was designed by local St. Cloud architectural firm Traynor, Hermanson and Hahn Architects in consultation St. Paul architect George Rafferty and liturgical consultant Frank Kacmarcik.

# ST. JOSEPH
# Sacred Heart Chapel

Architect: George Stauduhar, Rock Island, Illinois
Additions, renovations: Hammel, Green, and Abrahamson, Minneapolis, Ray Hermanson, St. Cloud
Consultant: Frank Kacmarcik
1912

On July 3, 1857, four Benedictine sisters and two candidates arrived in St. Cloud from St. Mary's Convent in Pennsylvania to teach the children of the ever-increasing German immigrants in Stearns County. Originally they were

members of St. Walburga's Convent in Eichstatt, Bavaria. The sisters lived and worked in St. Cloud for six years, but during that time struggled to establish themselves in the community. In 1863 they moved to St. Joseph at the request of the parish to teach in the local school. It was there that the community began to grow in both numbers and support. The sisters started a boarding school which over time evolved into what is today the College of St. Benedict. Over the ensuing years, the sisters staffed the numerous Catholic schools throughout the diocese and also engaged in the health-care ministry.

The growth in the convent and monastery led to planning for the present chapel in 1910. Groundbreaking took place in 1911, and the chapel was finished in 1914. Extensive renovations and additions were completed in 1983 including a gathering place, and reorienting the chapel so that the altar is under the dome and surrounded by seating on four sides.

## Architectural Description

Approaching the college town of St. Joseph, the tall cylindrical-based dome of Sacred Heart Chapel on the College of Saint Benedict's campus is a focal point in the skyline. Coming near the chapel's main entrance, the horizontality of the

recent addition with its flat roof balances the dark-burnished copper dome, and provides an architecturally compatible fit with the original chapel structure. The flat roof becomes background contrast and the smooth modernity of the light-beige brick walls uses proportions of plain wall surfaces modestly delineated with lines of offset brick that find compatibility with the surfaces of the original chapel.

Inside the new gathering space, a large skylight above a warm-toned wood light well amplifies the feeling of architectural comfort, and a pair of parallel colonnades, using columns removed for remodeling of the main chapel, establish connection in a minor sense with the original structure that leads from the gathering space.

The nave of the main worship space has been remodeled as part of the renovation program that built the gathering space. HGA Architects of Minneapolis, provided design documents for the project. The chapel's central dome constructed at mid-point over the barrel vault of the nave greatly amplifies the feeling of high space. Transepts that are both wide and shallow likewise extend horizontally at the intersection of the dome and barrel vault. The tremendous loads of these intersecting vaults holding a monumental dome receive a cluster of four columns in service to structural support, while standing in alignment with the colonnades under the barrel vault-work. Those columns, resting on Kasota stone bases, are large-scale smooth granite shafts with Corinthian capitals set below Classical Revival capitals. The nave walls feature engaged stone columns, and round arched windows contain translucent clear glazing, giving ample light to the cavernous interior.

Sacred Heart is distinctly different from the places of worship in the surrounding agrarian Stearns County countryside with its scattering of Gothic-Romanesque structures, whose architectural features seem almost delicate in comparison to this monumental and magnificent Classical Revival edifice.

## ST. NICHOLAS

# Church of St. Nicholas

Architect and Builder: Unknown

1914

### PARISH HISTORY

Immigrants from Luxemburg and the region around Trier, Germany settled this area in the early 1850s and built their first church on land donated by Nicholas Schmitt. The parish was named in honor of his patron saint.

As more settlers arrived, a decision was made to build a new and larger church. This decision created controversy within the parish between those who wanted this church built at the original site and those who wanted it built three miles to the southeast. Those who favored the new site argued that a new

parish recently formed at Cold Spring was only three miles away, and that the new St. Nicholas church should be moved to a more centralized location within the parish boundaries. In 1890 land was purchased further south, and plans drawn for the church. Still, many parishioners wanted to stay at the original site. At this point, the bishop put the parish under ecclesiastical censure. This meant that no masses or sacraments could be celebrated until the dispute was settled. Eventually, the new church was built on the recently purchased land. In 1914, this church burned to the ground. Plans started immediately for the present structure which was completed in 1915.

The site of the old Saint Nicholas church and cemetery was not forgotten, however. In 1935 a chapel was built there and named in honor of Our Lady of Perpetual Help. A fire in 1965 did considerable damage to the present church, but over the next several years the needed repairs to the interior were completed. Although many works of art were lost in the fire, the beautiful stained glass windows were saved.

## ARCHITECTURAL DESCRIPTION

The church of Saint Nicholas features a facade with a pair of bell towers, in similar fashion to several other Catholic churches in Stearns County. Here the tower shafts are wider than other such churches. These larger-scaled towers give a sense of strength that exemplifies the church's Romanesque Revival style. Tower corners have prominent buttresses, roof parapets rising above roof surfaces and sets of corbelling at tops of walls. Remnants of Gothic occur with pointed arch windows and steep roofs. Brick walls at Saint Nicholas have a notable feature rarely seen in area churches—Flemish bond brick pattern, in which brick units alternate length and width in repeating fashion. With this structure, the widths' darker color gives visual interest.

Saint Nicholas was built with a brick foundation rather than stone as used in earlier-built churches in Stearns County, although the brick face at the foundation is stepped out slightly as to simulate that aspect of typical stone foundations.

Inside the church's nave, the floor plan consists of a wide center aisle with narrow side aisles. Walls are of modest height compared to the lofty height of larger nineteenth-century Gothic churches. A somewhat shallow barrel vault that spans the nave from side wall to side wall, continuing this early twentieth-century's transition away from the Gothic toward full-fledged Romanesque. The church's main Gothic feature is the nave's pointed arch windows.

In a three-dimensional manner, pointed arches appear as space-created form, where transept vaulted ceilings intersect the nave ceiling, lending an immediately-apparent delightful feeling to the whole church interior. The

shape of these transept ceilings flows from round (at transept outer walls) to a flaring point where the ceilings intersect with each other well into the upper sides of the main barrel vault. This effect is heightened by the transepts' vaulted ceilings dramatically washed with sunlight coming from generous stained-glass windows, giving delightful play to these interior molded ceiling surfaces.

The altar area, though dramatically altered from the original by Vatican II, has a simplicity rendered by a plain back-altar table given backdrop by a painted wall panel bordered by a vertical series of gold triangles that flank a wood crucifix in the panel's center, crowned by a slightly-rounded edge triangle containing the top torso of Jesus Christ with outstretched hands.

# St. Rosa
# Church of St. Rose of Lima

Architect: Leo Schaefer, additions and renovation
Builder: Unknown
1882–1921

## Parish History

The township in which St. Rosa is located was officially established in 1871 and called Millwood, probably for the large stands of forest which covered the area at the time. Early settlers in the St. Rosa area had to travel nearly ten miles to Freeport to attend mass which was a hardship, especially during the winter

months. The desire to form their own parish and build a church led to the formation of a committee to ask for the assistance of Father Maehren, pastor of Sacred Heart at Freeport to assist them. St. Rosa became a mission of Freeport, and the first masses were held in the homes of the parishioners.

In 1904, St. Rose got its first resident pastor, and land was donated for a church. Wishing to have their church on a hill, the parishioners hauled in large amounts of dirt, raising the elevation of the land by several feet. The long awaited goal came quickly when Sacred Heart at Freeport completed a new and larger church, and their older frame structure was moved to the building site at St. Rosa. At the time, it had no steeple or bell. During the ensuing months, it was brick veneered by the parishioners, who hauled the brick in wagons from the railroad station in Freeport. In 1921 a bell tower and sacristies were added and in 1971 the interior was renovated.

## ARCHITECTURAL DESCRIPTION

Situated on a small rise of land formed when the church structure was moved to the once-flat site, Saint Rose of Lima's high-roofed structure and its tall steeple render the church a prominent presence for the houses and storefronts in the small settlement of Saint Rosa. Approach to the entrance comes by a long sidewalk lined both sides with cedar trees. The exterior is a well-composed example of standard Gothic-Romanesque traits: steep-pitched roof, square bell tower with steeple centered on the front façade, round arched windows along yellow brick nave walls, and stepped brick corbelling at tops of gable walls. However, the exterior of Saint Rose reveals a subtle variation of Gothic-Romanesque details: a gable slightly projecting from the bell tower, and thin corner pilasters rising up to the shaft's crested wall parapet that are similar to the narrow pilasters on the nave walls.

In the interior, an elongated barrel vault interspersed with thin ribs springing from a mildly ornamented entablature forms the ceiling of Saint Rose. Engaged columns with Ionic gilded capitals line the nave walls in simulated support of the entablature. The columns' inset panels feature stencil bands in the same pattern as those that outline the round arch separating the nave from the sanctuary. A three-step platform brings the altar table slightly forward into the nave floor area. Behind the altar, a stepped wall built into the rear wall holds a small tabernacle and a simple crucifix.

## ST. STEPHEN

# Church of St. Stephen

Architect: John Jager, Minneapolis
Builder: unknown
1903

### PARISH HISTORY

When Father Pierz arrived in central Minnesota in 1853 and saw the suitability of the land for farming, he wrote back to his native Slovenians urging them to come to the area. He had no takers, and instead enlisted German immigrants to come to the area. On a visit to his homeland in 1864, he was more successful, and the immigrants began to come to the area around St. Stephen making it the first Slovenian settlement in the United States. Later that year, Gregor Pogacnik and Gregor Peternell claimed land and built log cabins in the area that was to be called St. Stephen.

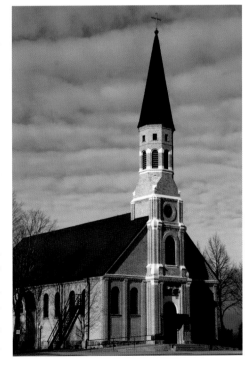

Upon his return to central Minnesota Father Pierz also brought back several missionaries to help him in his work with the Indian missions he had established in the areas north of St. Cloud and as far up as Crow Wing near Brainerd. One of these priests, Father Buh, offered the first mass at St. Stephen in the Woods, as the settlement was often called, in the home of Gregor Pogacnik in 1867. Father Buh was also responsible for organizing the parish in 1870. Plans were soon made to build a church, a log structure measuring thirty by fifty feet was to serve the parish until the present church was completed in

1904. Masses were held on a monthly basis until 1875 when more regular services could be held. By 1901 there were seventy families in the congregation, and at this time , Father John Trobec took on the task of building the present church. The parishioners donated a great deal of the labor, hauling rocks from nearby farms for the foundation, and later brick made at the old kiln in St. Cloud and shipped as far as Rice, about ten miles northeast of St. Stephen. When the church was dedicated in October of 1904, it had been only partially furnished. The pews extended only to the middle of the church, and there were no bells in the tower. After three more years of fund raising, the bells had been purchased, and by 1913 the pipe organ was installed. Over the next twenty years, more improvements were made including a complete redecorating of the interior by Gosar, a Slovenian artist from Pennsylvania. Gosar also painted twenty-six murals on canvas which were then glued to the ceiling. The church and rectory were placed on the National Register of Historic Places in 1982.

## ARCHITECTURAL DESCRIPTION

Saint Stephen's exterior follows the typical architectural features seen in many of the Catholic churches of Stearns County. Jager designed the church with a relatively steep-pitched gable roof, yellow-beige brick walls punctuated with round arched windows along the nave wall, a square bell tower centered on the façade that transitions to a octagonal shaft supporting a tall slender spire, all designed with simplicity and subtle proportion. Local sources have commented that parishioners instructed Jager to design a church with walls not as high as typical churches in order to keep construction costs down, but the steeple should be high enough so people could be sure to see it from a good distance away. True to their wishes, like so many other churches in rural Stearns County, Saint Stephen's central location in this town of 900 people serves as a landmark for miles around. The church today is very much unaltered from its original construction.

The design of the church's interior reflects the apparent Eastern European tradition for barrel-vaulted ceilings. Somewhat shallow bands demarcate the ceiling's half-round curve into several sections. Eastern European churches also favor a relatively simple interior with ornamental features concentrated in specific areas such as the altars, stained-glass windows, Stations of the Cross and a few other locations that make the most of where the eye needs to focus.

The sanctuary presents itself slightly behind a large semi-circular arch serving as a terminus for the nave. A Vatican II style altar is positioned in front of the main altar which remains intact, as if patiently waiting for its assumption to re-use. The front panel of the altar features a sculptured relief panel of the Last Supper with figures representing Christ and the apostles in whitish garments with deep folds that accentuate shadows.

Above and slightly behind the altar, a tri-partite reredo composed of columns supporting a pair of arched highly stylized entablatures flanks a more prominent and taller structure whose open front holds a crucifix. This ornate assembly is painted white with heavily gilded ornament that outlines the architectural elements—all set within a shallow arched recess whose outer edges are tipped with gold-painted radiating finger-like shapes. Surrounding the arch is a flat-faced panel with painted figures of angels and saints in a blue sky background, all revealing a heaven awaiting parishioners.

## ST. WENDEL

# Church of St. Columbkille

Congregation Built
1877

### PARISH HISTORY

Irish settlers were the first to reach the area around St. Wendel, and they named their settlement Maples because of the numerous stands of maple trees in the vicinity. In 1867, two of the early settlers, Barney Murphy and Angus Wilson visited the abbot at St. John's to ask for a priest to say mass and administer sacraments. The first priest to minister to the settlers was Father Cornelius Wittman, but within a year the abbey sent an Irish priest, Father Augustine

147

Burns. For several years these visits by the Benedictines were on a monthly basis. In fact, Maples would not get a resident pastor until 1906.The log schoolhouse was used for worship for several years until 1877 when a wood-framed church measuring thirty-six by forty-eight feet was dedicated. This structure had no steeple, but was painted white so that it would be recognized as a church.

Their church was called St. Columbkille's for a sixth-century Irish missionary who spent his life spreading the gospel in Northern England in what is now Scotland. The parish continued to be served by Benedictine priests until 1891, and, following that, by Diocesan clergy. At this time the parish consisted of only sixteen families, but after the turn of the century, more settlers arrived most of whom were of German, Polish, and Slovenian ancestry.

St. Columbkille's celebrated the completion of a steeple and installation of a bell on their church in 1903, and in the ensuing years several other building projects were undertaken. In 1927, the interior was renovated, which included vaulting the ceiling of the nave. In the 1930s, the church was raised, and a basement was added. The excavation was done by hand with volunteer help.

St. Columbkille's is the only wood-framed Catholic church in continuous use in Stearns County.

## ARCHITECTURAL DESCRIPTION

The Church of Saint Columbkille's exterior wood siding makes this place of worship the only wood-clad Catholic church in the county, and also probably the smallest. Its architectural lineage goes back to New England Gothic-inspired wood frame churches, with typical narrow-lap white-painted siding, simple rectangular bell tower with a tall pointed spire placed squarely to project from the façade, with its lower section serving as a vestibule.

The nave's oval-shaped clear-span ceiling rises gently to its center and curves downward to join nave side walls, which are clad with twelve-inch square acoustic panels. Narrow stained-glass windows along the side walls extend their Gothic arched heads above typical wall height and into the ceiling curve, making flared-inward pointed hood shapes. With the intimate and simple character of this space, these seemingly minor elements contribute subtle architecturally enhancing detail that enhances Saint Columbkille's interior. These Gothic arch flared window heads also relate to the three much larger pointed arches in the wall separating the nave from the sanctuary. The center arch, which opens to the sanctuary space, is larger than the two flanking arches that are inset shapes within the wall.

The sanctuary apse space contains a similar-shaped arch panel applied to the rear wall. On both sides of the panel, varnished wood paneling with vertical thin battens covers the bottom half of the wall. A small crucifix is attached to the center arched panel. The altar is made from a horizontal wood top supported by two block shapes whose faces slant slightly inward toward a center narrow open space.

This interior architectural character at Saint Columbkille is a composition of minimal shapes, unified within a white enclosure that achieves small-scaled composition with harmony, balance, and simple elegance—all without a stick of ornament. Function is unified by form here, a feat to which all architecture aspires.

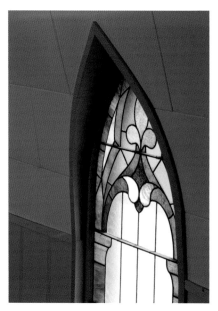

## SAUK CENTRE
# Church of Our Lady of the Angels

Architects: Cordella and Olson, Minneapolis
Builder: Edward Hirt and Son, St. Cloud
1925

### PARISH HISTORY

The vast majority of settlers coming to Stearns County in the latter half of the nineteenth-century were of German descent; however, there were significant numbers of other nationalities as well, including Irish. Such was the case in Sauk Centre, and the desire of the Irish to worship in a church where sermons and prayers were given in English led to the formation of Our Lady of the Angels parish in 1883. Previously, the Irish settlers were members of the predominantly German-speaking St. Paul's parish that had been formed in 1871.

The fifteen families making up the nucleus of the new parish wasted no time in building their first church. A frame structure seating 150 was completed in less than a year from the date of the founding of the parish. Getting their own pastor was much more difficult, however. In the early years, mass and sacraments were offered by Father Gamache, pastor of St. Patrick's, the Irish Catholic church in nearby Melrose. It wasn't until 1895 that Father John Fitzgerald became the first resident pastor of the parish. Father John Fearing arrived in 1917 and served until 1932, the longest of any pastor in the history of the parish.

On Christmas Day in 1924, following Christmas services, the frame church burned to the ground. A committee was quickly formed to plan the construction of a new church. A building fund had been set up previously which totaled $16,000, and within a week after the fire, parishioners had pledged another $9,000. Construction began in 1925, and on March 28, 1926, the present Romanesque Basilica style church was dedicated. At the time of its dedication it was noted that this church "has no comparison to others in the area in architectural correctness and beauty."

## ARCHITECTURAL DESCRIPTION

The exterior of Our Lady of the Angels reveals its architects, Cordella and Olson exploring an architectural shift from the traditional Romanesque motifs towards what might be described as "Free-Romanesque," re-arranging traditional features, such as shallow roof pitch, moving the bell tower towards the rear of the nave, eliminating the Gothic-influenced tall slender spire and minimizing ornament. In this respect, Cordella and Olson moved Catholic church architecture forward into the twentieth century by reclaiming its fifth- and sixth-century early Romanesque features, seen frequently in Byzantine churches.

The nave of Our Lady of the Angels is flanked with side aisles with round columns capped with ornate Corinthian capitals supporting simple-surfaced round arches. Above, the side walls of the apse have round clerestory windows with stained glass featuring geometric cross motifs. The nave's coffered ceiling has elongated rectangular panels.

The most eye-arresting feature of the church's interior is the semi-circular apse, composed of a partial circular colonnade, called an ambulatory, set a few feet inward from the apse's smoothly curved exterior wall. The six simple round columns, made of marble from Sienna, Italy, capped with Corinthian capitals, render the apse with a measure of embellishment against the alabaster purity of the apse wall. Above the colonnade, the partial dome ceiling features a stylized painting of the Blessed Virgin floating amid golden-brown-tinged clouds accompanied by cherubs. Sauk Centre artist Roger Reinardy created this painting in 2004 based on a work by eighteenth century Italian painter Giambattista Tiepolo. Reinardy captured a modern sense of realism with rich red garment folds highlighted by deep shadows in the swirling robes of the Blessed Virgin.

The marble altar table surface is capped by a back ledge with a molded cap. The principal materials are Tennessee and Italian marble. A central tabernacle pediment features a roof canopy supported by engaged marble columns similar to the apse. Above the altar tabernacle, eight round columns support a baldachin-like dome clad with half-round gilded lapping shingles. On both sides are projecting pedestals with statues of kneeling angels holding trumpets. The altar and Stations of the Cross were designed by Cordella and Olson, architects in Minneapolis and built by St. Paul Statuary.

## SAUK CENTRE
# Church of St. Paul
Architect: Guido Beck, Dubuque, Iowa
Builders: Paul Koshiol, St. Cloud; foundations
Carl Kropp, Edward Hirt, St. Cloud; superstructure
1904

### PARISH HISTORY

The city of Sauk Centre, located along Interstate 94 in the northwest corner of Stearns County, was immortalized by author Sinclair Lewis in his novel *Main Street*. Its early settlers were Yankees who built businesses around a fort which had been used as a refuge during the Indian Uprising of 1862. The

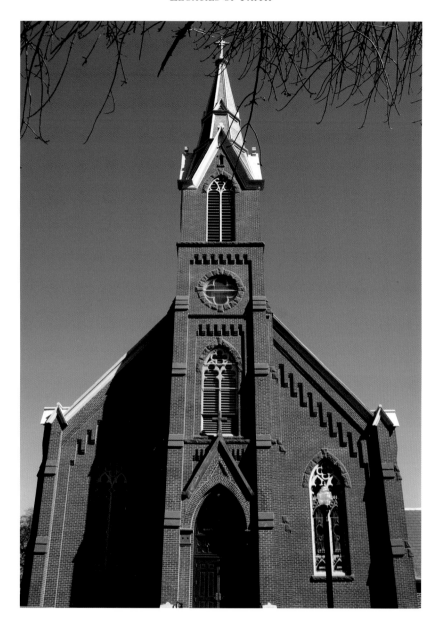

earliest churches in the town were Protestant serving the spiritual needs of its earliest inhabitants.

German Catholic settlers arrived in the early 1860s. Records indicate that the first mass celebrated in Sauk Centre was in 1864 in the home of Joseph Casper. A number of missionary priests came to the area over the next few years, usually at monthly intervals, to say mass in the homes of the settlers. St. Paul's parish was formed in 1870, and in the following year the first frame church was built. An increasing number of Catholics coming to the area necessitated an addition to the church in 1886. In 1883 the parish received its first resident pastor, but in the same year, a group of Irish families broke away from St. Paul's to form their own parish, Our Lady of the Angels. St. Paul's, however, grew steadily, and in 1899 a fund-raising campaign was initiated to build a new church. This Gothic style structure was dedicated in 1906 and continues to serve the parish at the present time.

## ARCHITECTURAL DESCRIPTION

The Church of Saint Paul faithfully expresses the Gothic standards of architectural verticality with façade elements that outline its brick massing. The tall bell tower with its slender spire projects from the center of the façade and is balanced by flanking steep-pitched roofs with pronounced cornices and stepped arched corbelling. A tall Gothic arched stained-glass window is centered in the bell tower above a gable roof covering the entry doorway, and the single Gothic

arched stained-glass windows set somewhat lower in each of the flanking façade walls form a tripartite pattern that repeats in other façade elements.

The interior of Saint Paul is characterized by a straight-walled nave that is unbroken by any projecting transepts and contains Gothic arched stained-glass windows. A vaulted nave ceiling clear spans from side wall to side wall, terminating at an arched wall opening to the sanctuary and the apse beyond. A five-sided vaulted ceiling covers the apse. A gold-tinted band marks the curved face of the arched wall opening, and a series of similar narrow bands outline the apse's segmented vaults, all gently bending over the immense and intricate reredos that becomes the architectural centerpiece of the entire interior. An elaborately detailed wood-faced altar forms the base of this magnificence.

Hyper-Gothic might be an apt term to describes this carved wood fren-zy, a construction of varnished wood spiky mini-spires, copiously detailed, reaching above tripartite open-faced vertical vaults—the larger center one holding a crucifix attended by standing statues of female figures, and on either side are smaller chambers which display St. Joseph and St. Paul. Elaborate wood detail rims these openings with slender engaged columns supporting intensely decorative arch-work over the face of each opening. The higher peaks of the reredos contain red-robed statues of saints surrounded by elabo-rate woodwork. Adding to the reredos, a pair of tall stained-glass Gothic arched windows in two angled faces of the apse deliver a refreshing sense of color to the space.

Of special interest is Christ on the crucifix—brown body with black hair, not the typical pale skin and brown hair seen in many Northern European and Upper Midwest American churches. The Church of Saint Paul's 1904 construction occurred while the Romanesque influence was well under-way in nearby churches, but this place of worship held to its Gothic forebear-er.

Simple · Elegant · Sensitive

# SPRING HILL
# Church of St. Michael
Architect: George Bergmann, St. Cloud
1900

## PARISH HISTORY

Most of the early settlement in Stearns County took place in areas to the south and west of St. Cloud toward what is now Cold Spring, and on to Richmond, St. Martin, and Spring Hill. This is probably because of the abundant water supply in the many lakes and rivers, and also because it was the

path of the Red River Oxcart Trail used to carry furs and supplies between Pembina in North Dakota and St. Paul. By 1855 Father Pierz had already visited the area of Spring Hill to offer mass in the home of one of the settlers, Xavier Poepping. In 1857 Father Clement Staub visited the settlement and offered Mass. He is credited with the official organization of the parish in 1858. It has been recounted how he walked from Richmond nearly ten miles to Spring Hill to offer mass for the families in the area.

The first church at Spring Hill was a log structure built in 1864, and used until it burned down in 1871. A large framed church was built on the site of the present church, and a small hamlet grew up around it. The parish received its first resident pastor, Father Ambrose Lethert, in 1879. Shortly following his arrival, the area was beset with a smallpox epidemic. In all, twenty people died and many more became ill from the disease. Father Lethert was remembered for his tireless work among the stricken parishioners. He went from home to home nursing the sick and bringing food. He also built coffins for the deceased and dug the graves. The grave markers of the victims can be seen in the cemetery which is immediately in back of the present church.

In 1899 a fire of unknown origin destroyed both the frame church and the adjacent rectory. Planning for the present brick Romanesque-style church started immediately. Granite for the foundation, taken from nearby outcroppings, was cut and dressed by the parishioners, and brick was hauled from the brickyard in Meire Grove. By 1902 the basement was ready for services, and the completed church was dedicated in 1903. In 1946 a tornado struck the church, causing major roof and water damage. Through the great financial sacrifice of the parishioners, repairs and restoration were completed at a cost of

thirty-seven thousand dollars which was more than the total cost of the church when it was originally built.

## ARCHITECTURAL DESCRIPTION

Saint Michael's is a simple and elegant representation of Gothic-Romanesque church architecture. The style uses the steep-pitched gabled roof with raised parapets and tall slender tower and spire from the Gothic tradition, and infuses a sense of solidity with half-round arch motifs in façade treatment and window heads, and corbel features that emphasize structure.

The lesson Saint Michaels offers is how

tradition can be maintained by faithfully following an architectural style, keeping the design wholly within the style's attributes, and creating quality by skillful proportion of design elements, giving detail in a subtle and sensitive manner where it gives optimal reinforcement to major features.

These design elements that contribute to its quality are the stone caps that outline principal architectural features contrasting their light beige color with the red brick that clads the building, the bell tower's half-round

162

arches and the hexagonal tapered steeple's graceful transition to a roofed square base atop the brick bell tower.

To amplify the architectural presence of St. Michael, a long straight path leading to the main entrance is lined symmetrically with two straight rows of trees, planted close enough together to form a leafy canopy for parishioners on their way to the entrance—a remarkable site feature occasionally employed in renown works of architecture uniting landscape and structure.

Saint Michael's interior features a nave—consisting of a center aisle aligned with the axis of the sanctuary, and minor aisles bordered by rows of columns set away from the side walls. The columns' simple square shape with subtle corner molding is translated into column capitals, likewise square, with flared sides form-

ing decorous Corinthian capitals. From these columns, a series of intersecting vaults spring in modulated rhythm across the nave, in perfect pitch composing a sonorous architectural composition.

In so many Catholic churches, there is no greater area of concentrated architecture than the altar and its exuberantly structured backdrop. This is especially true at Saint Michael's; a highly articulated altar is set between a pair of arches on embellished columns, the smaller ensemble stepped back from the front set. All surfaces are varnished wood with intricate details tipped in gold. Within the arches and columns are pedestals holding polychromed statues arranged on both sides of a crucifix. The whole complex is free standing, as are the columns and statues, from the half-circular apse.

But the most dramatic aspect of the structure is the statue of Saint

Michael, known to Catholics as an archangel, with military-like powers charged to rescue the faithful from the enemy. Poised on top of the baldachin, Saint Michael, with his gold-edged wings at his back, holds his sword in his right hand at his side, while his outstretched left hand holds a set of scales. He appears on one hand ready to protect, and on the other hand available to measure justice.

# WAITE PARK
# Church of St. Joseph
1916–1918
Architect: unknown
Builder: unknown

## PARISH HISTORY

The city of Waite Park, located on the west edge of St. Cloud, was named for Henry Waite, a local lawyer and business man. The growth he envisioned for the area came as a result of two industries, the Great Northern Railroad, which had a rail car-building facility there, and the granite quarries that employed half of the local residents at the turn of the twentieth century. The town grew from a population of 500 in 1897 to 1,800 in 1915.

Catholics in Waite Park were attending church in St. Cloud and St. Joseph until 1915 when the diocese sent Father Charles Grunenwald to explore the idea of organizing a parish. On January 1, 1916, the parish was officially incorporated and named for St. Joseph, the patron saint of workmen. The first mass, celebrated on July 4, was held outdoors at the site where the first church was to be built. It also included a fair and bazaar at which $3,000 was raised.

When the church was completed in 1916, the parish numbered sixty-five families, and within two years this number had nearly doubled. In 1918 the church was remodeled, adding a transept and bell tower. A tornado in May of 1938 greatly damaged the church, and initially it was thought that it would need to be torn down. Through the hard work and diligence of the parishioners, a method was found to save the structure by the addition of steel girders. The whole parish was involved in the rebuilding—from the structural work to the interior cleaning and painting The remodeling was completed in the fall of 1938 and the church is still in use today.

## ARCHITECTURAL DESCRIPTION

The Church of Saint Joseph is a departure from the typical brick Gothic-Romanesque religious edifice found in Stearns County. Stucco is its exterior material, and its architectural style is a variant of English-influenced Late-Gothic Revival, which appeared throughout the nation near the end of the nineteenth century. Saint Joseph's exterior displays two of that style's main attributes: a square bell tower and an exaggerated steep gabled roof. The bell tower is semi-attached to one side of the nave, featuring a flat roof girded by a crenelated (castle-like series of open spaces between raised battlements) parapet. The steep roof becomes a major architectural statement.

The interior expands a greater sense of English-influenced Late-Gothic Revival. The nave's exposed ceiling trusses, gambrel-shaped (similar to barn roofs), somewhat heavy members in dark finished wood, are formed with series of vertical scroll-cut struts that are emblematic of that style. White walls give strong contrast to dark finished wood trim throughout the interior, especially in Saint Joseph's wide and deep transept wings, which furthers the Late English Gothic character. That style also can be seen in the rectangular-shaped stained-glass windows, containing simple rectangular patterns of pale yellow-white glass without liturgical symbols.

The flat rear sanctuary wall holds long vertical banners of varying lengths from a cross beam affixed to the wall, surmounted by a simple crucifix. Bands of stenciling course through wall surfaces and provide subtle reinforcement to the predominate interior dark wood members.

The English-inspired Gothic Revival at Saint Joseph is an anomaly to the almost-ubiquitous German Gothic architecture of preceding eras, throughout the region. Reasons for this are not known at this time, but the church's 1916 to 1918 time of construction came when the German Gothic style, as well as traditional architecture of all types, had nearly run its course. This allowed an in-between time, for experiment with various revival styles to be put into eclectic exercise in the county before American-based styles, such as the Prairie Movement that led to Early Modernism, gained national favor.

PART TWO

# The Modern Churches
1941-2000

By the late 1940s and early 1950s, the stand-alone church building no longer could provide the increasing needs for many communities. In response to demographic shifts and parishioners melding their secular middle class lives with commitment to their faith, parish leaders established planning processes for new facilities. The architecture of these buildings centered around multi-use complexes, integrating worship spaces with "gathering spaces," expanded administrative facilities, elementary schools accompanied by gymnasiums and other uses. Religion had come to accommodate social aspects of parishioners' lives that found consonance with the Catholic faith. Unlike the fixed and permanent-aspect of the architecture of traditional churches, these new building complexes planned for built-in flexibility to anticipate future changes, in ways that the nineteenth century churches had no reason to provide.

The effect on the architectural character of the church space was transformative. With modernism already displacing ornament as a means to amplify the religious experience, the design of the nave sought to create plain surfaces and exposed structural members to create space that essentially became a renewal of Catholicism's traditional purpose–concentrating the faithful on the altar and the celebration of mass. In a comprehensive sense, the exterior and interior of these places, including the worship space, took on a sense of the secular. Their architectural identity, characterized by their one-level horizontality, seems to have taken cues from the concurrent development of mid-twentieth century public school buildings, libraries, hospitals, office buildings and government facilities. Invariably, the architecture of these new religious structures became place centered rather than the iconic base for the community. In other words, the horizontally-oriented buildings covered a substantially larger land area than the surrounding houses and commercial buildings. As a result, these new religious complexes were built at the outer edges of the growing community and away from the dense older central core. Adjoining the mid-century surroundings, these religious structures gained an appropriate identity as modern religious places. In an ironic sense, the town's tallest elevated structure, the municipal water tank, became the highest local landmark, displacing the much more narrow church spire.

## BELGRADE

# Church of
# St. Francis de Sales

Contractor: Math Worms Construction, New Munich
1956

### PARISH HISTORY

The town of Belgrade, located in the southwestern corner of Stearns County, came into being with the construction of the Soo Line Railroad through the area in 1886. Its name was given by the surveyor of the town site, a man of Serbian descent. By 1890 the population had grown to 300 people as Belgrade became the trade center for the surrounding area.

The earliest Catholic settlers attended church in Spring Hill, nearly ten miles away, but soon they requested that a priest visit their settlement. The pastor at Spring Hill offered the first masses in Belgrade in the upstairs room of the bank. The first wood-frame church was completed in 1890, and enlarged in 1897 due to growth in the area. In the mid 1930s, the church was completely remodeled including the installation of a hand-carved high altar which had been crafted in Germany. This church continued to serve the parish until 1957 when the present structure was dedicated.

The new church included both a worship space and an attached parsonage. The high altar from the old church is installed here, and a mural entitled *The Glorification of the Eucharist*, which was painted in Rome, hangs in the sanctuary. Also of note are the stained-glass windows above and behind the altar depicting angels with the symbols of the Blessed Sacrament.

## ARCHITECTURAL DESCRIPTION

The Church of Saint Francis deSales is part of a building complex in a residential neighborhood that contains a modestly scaled church connected to an administrative link, which is joined by a priest's residence with an attached one-car garage. The architectural components are unified by brick walls in

light brown and slightly orange-tint. Hip roofs on the residence and administrative section complement the low-gabled roof on the church. The overall
effect is this religious facility fitting well into a residential neighborhood.

Similar to other early modern churches, a wide series of doors with
large glass panels leads parishioners into a wide low-ceilinged vestibule with
a similarly expansive set of doors opening to the church's nave. A progression
of laminated structural members forming columns attached to the nave walls
gracefully curve upwards into rafters, and are joined just below the ridgeline
with horizontal crossbars, all supporting a knotty pine paneled ceiling. Lower
interior wall surfaces along the side and rear have brick wainscoting with
white painted concrete block above. The rectangular-shaped nave demarcates
itself from the sanctuary with narrow sections of brick walls flanking the opening to the altar platform, giving the sanctuary a somewhat narrower volume
than the nave. These walls have a Flemish bond brick pattern, in which typical brick lengths alternate with end faces that, in this case, project outward
slightly, and the orangish-red color of these masonry units contributes an
interesting subtle texture to the church's interior.

The 1956 construction date indicates that this structure was built less
than a decade before Vatican II, and the somewhat deep recess of the sanctuary
may have held the traditional altar with a typical ornate background structure.
Typical to Vatican II proscriptions, the altar now is a table enabling the mass
celebrants to face the faithful. The wall behind features an elegant composition

of wood panels with a series of vertical strips separating simulated gothic embellishments near the panel tops, with the center section rising slightly higher than the side sections. This intricate wood articulation is surmounted by a tall painting within a wooden frame, reaching the ceiling. Titled *The Glorification of the Eucharist*, this work of art was painted in Rome and donated by a parishioner. It depicts a Christ figure holding an opened book, surrounded by infant angels, all rendered in rich color tones with expert detail. The total effect draws the eye deep into the nave interior, the whole of which composes simplicity with a sense of comfortable space, given well-appointed enrichment.

## Brooten

# Church of St. Donatus

Architects: Fr. Maurice Landwehr, Roger Landwehr
Builder: Oscar Terhaar Construction, Brooten
1966

### Parish History

The town of Brooten, located in the western-most edge of Stearns County near the Pope County line, had a few settlers as early as 1859. However, during the Dakota Uprising of 1862, they moved away, returning in 1864. The first real growth in the area did not occur until 1886 when the Soo Line Railroad came through the area.

Before 1900 the few Catholics who had settled there were of Irish descent and attended church in nearby Belgrade and Padua. The first services in Brooten took place in 1908 in the old schoolhouse. The first church was built in 1911 and furnished over several years. It was named St. Donatus for a Roman soldier martyred in about 173 A.D. The parish was considered a mission, being served by priests from nearby parishes until 1919 when the first resident pastor arrived. Over the years the parish has grown, but still remains relatively small. The present church was built in 1966 and dedicated in 1967.

### Architectural Features

The Church of Saint Donatus represents ecclesiastical modern architectural design prevalent in the mid 1960s: modest height walls, a low-pitched roof with its front gable overhang slightly flared forward, and exterior stone walls. The gran-

ite came from local quarries, dressed to a coarse surface finish, and cut into long modular blocks of varying heights and lengths and laid in random coursing, with some slightly projecting units. The entrance is intentionally modest with narrow vertical floor-to-ceiling windows filled with bright stained-glass components bordering the doors. A cupola-type element with a square low base faced

177

with louvers supports a low-pitched hip roof whose corners slightly flare outward. A spire above is made of two sharply pitched intersecting flat-faced triangles, rendering a modernist interpretation of the traditional spire.

The 1960s modern vocabulary carries through the interior. Clear spanning steel beams, wrapped in wood facing, taper somewhat diminutively toward the ceiling ridge line. These beams extend downward to become legs, attached to exterior nave walls, tapering outward to join the deepest beam profile—a very modernist motif. The exterior façade's granite is exposed in the vestibule, as well as flanking a wall grid between the vestibule and the nave.

White painted plaster walls serve a similar flanking function to the opening between the nave and the narrower sanctuary. To the left, facing the altar, the wall wraps along the side of the sanctuary to enclose a confessional and a sacristy. On the right, the wall enclosure separates the sanctuary from a choir area and the organ. The walls of each enclosure facing the sanctuary feature another widely employed modern feature—an assembly of vertical and deep wood members, spaced apart with flat wood infill panels that integrate openings between the spaces on both sides.

Stack bond concrete blocks form side nave walls, and their white painted surface corresponds to the white plaster ceiling between the beams, giving appropriate contrast to the granite, glass, and wood. Here modernism works at its best—generating depth with layers of form, space, and color in intriguing architectural design.

# COLD SPRING

# Assumption Chapel
### 1952

Compared to typical chapels, Assumption Chapel is quite small. This stone structure's interior width measures barely more than two side-by-side persons' outstretched arms, and the exterior roof ridge is approximately twenty-two feet in height. It is located on a hilltop in a grove of oak trees at the edge of Cold Spring, accessed by a narrow winding road. The interior walls are faced with polished granite and the sloped ceiling uses exposed redwood beams and red-wood paneling. A granite altar becomes the interior focal point, and a statue of the Blessed Mother stands above.

The chapel's former name, the Grasshopper Chapel, reveals its history. In the late 1870s, a ferocious grasshopper plague infested the local countryside, attacking meadows and especially farm fields, causing crop failures and threatening the local economy. With no insecticides then available, farmers' attempts to eradicate them by laborious methods such as dragging large tar-covered sheets nailed to runners across the fields, collecting the grasshoppers in hooped burlap bags were ineffective. The farmers' strong religious beliefs looked to prayer as a solution, which they did with great fervor. This extraordinary plague caused them to call on Governor John S. Pillsbury to declare a day of prayer, which he set for April 26, 1877. In July of that year, the community started construction of a wood-framed chapel. A short time after that, the grasshoppers disappeared.

In 1894, the chapel was destroyed by a tornado. In 1952, a new chapel was built and dedicated to the Assumption of the Blessed Mother, a Catholic holy day. Assumption Chapel is used for diocese religious events and has become a tourist attraction.

At night, this vaguely Gothic style structure is illuminated with spotlights, giving visibility to the town below the hill. According to local legend, a man once left a local tavern and drove down a nearby road, looked up, saw the illuminated chapel, returned to the tavern and declared to the patrons: "Anytime you see a church flying through the air, it's time to stop drinking."

COLD SPRING

# Church of St. Boniface

Architect: Ray Hermanson, St. Cloud
Builder: Loeffel–Engstrand, Stillwater
1978

## PARISH HISTORY

The city of Cold Spring developed and grew because of its location on the Sauk River where a dam had been built to provide energy for mills and because of the granite quarries which developed into an industry that remains vibrant today. A Catholic parish wasn't easily established because of the proximity of churches in St. Nicholas and Jacob's Prairie.

In 1878 a group of local citizens succeeded in receiving permission to build a church, and in that same year St. Boniface was born, named for the patron saint of Germany. Also in 1878 a basement church was constructed which was used until 1884 when a large Romanesque structure was completed.

The parish put a high priority on the education of its youth, building an elementary school in 1916 and high school in 1926. In the 1970s the parish embarked on a program to expand and build new parish facilities culminating

in the construction of the present church in 1978. The old church remained, and was used as a parish hall until 2003 when it was torn down. The present complex is very impressive and includes an elementary school, a parish center, and the church, which seats 1,000 people.

## ARCHITECTURAL DESCRIPTION

The Church of Saint Boniface occupies a prominent site and forms a major component in the parishes' multi-use complex. Its tall square bell tower—a unique feature in contemporary church design—serves minimalist architecture as a landmark for the community. The walls of the one level building sections are random ashlar stone, joined in some areas with modular granite blocks that lend variety to the building massing.

The interior of Saint Boniface features large wide-span scissors type trusses, giving generous sloped ceiling space to the nave. These structural members rest on massive wood-faced beams approximately five feet in vertical dimension, symbolic in their own way in which modern religious architecture formed structure to guide faith, in place what plaster-molded ornament worked to do several decades before. The altar sits on a platform thrust outward from the back wall, which is composed of a series of white wall planes that give contrast to the architectural composition. Granite pavers add subtle texture and variety. As typical of modern churches in the region, wood pews and various trim members are finished with a clear varnish, giving a warm tint, and with the honey-hued knotty pine ceiling decking, the large space takes on variety and architectural interest.

## COLLEGEVILLE

# St. John's Abbey

Architect: Marcel Breuer, New York

1961

As noted in the introduction of this book, the Benedictine Order has contributed significantly to the religious and economic formation of Stearns
County, beginning in 1856 and most actively continuing today. The university campus probably has more buildings of excellent architecture, designed by
architects with national and international renown, than any other institute of

learning in Minnesota. Foremost among these superb structures is Saint John's Abbey Church, built in 1961, and frequently noted as one of the most remarkable buildings in the history of modern architecture. It was designed by one of the most influential architects of the twentieth century, Marcel Breuer.

A remarkable aspect of Saint John's comes from its planning before, but in anticipation of Vatican II, which required no changes to the church after the norms were issued.

Breuer's design of the abbey church represents this architect's role in modern architecture's dogmatism of enhancing human aspirations where structure itself, in a relatively pure, unornamented expression, provides enveloping shelter that forms its own aesthetic. Breuer advances this ideal further with Saint

John's Abbey Church, by employing the process of poured concrete into massive carpenter-constructed wooden board forms that shape concrete into architectural expression of function and spirit. The wood forms were oiled to make release of each board easier when the concrete became solid, and the grain pattern of the boards is imprinted in the concrete components.

Saint John's Abbey church continued Breuer's experiment with poured concrete in his 1953 design of the UNESCO headquarters in New York. Breuer created the assembly space with walls and roof becoming one continuous folded plate concrete structure, in which the geometry of folded shapes cover a large floor area unimpeded with columns.

Outside the entry to the church, a poured concrete bell banner in the form of a thin slab on pylons holds a cross and five bells. Just inside the church, an expansive free-standing concrete balcony provides a sculptural statement to the expansive interior. Above the balcony, a stained-glass window made of hexagonal concrete cells containing abstract glass panels of brilliant blues and reds spreads across the façade and enlivens the gray concrete surfaces. The window was designed by Saint John's art professor Bronislaw Bok, and was fabricated by monks, students, faculty, and many volunteers. Passing under the low ceiling of the balcony, the dramatic interior opens to view. The altar, centered in the nave, occupies a large brick-surfaced platform; overhead a white flat-formed baldachin, tethered with guy wires, seems to float effortlessly in the awe-inspiring space.

## GREENWALD

# Church of St. Andrew

Architect: Frank Jackson, St. Cloud
Builder: Conlon Construction, St. Cloud
1923–1941

### PARISH HISTORY

St. Andrew's is the youngest parish in rural Stearns County, established in 1923. Prior to that year, residents attended St. John the Baptist parish in nearby Meire Grove. How the town of Greenwald came to have its own parish is of interest here because it illustrates the influence of the railroads in the growth of towns.

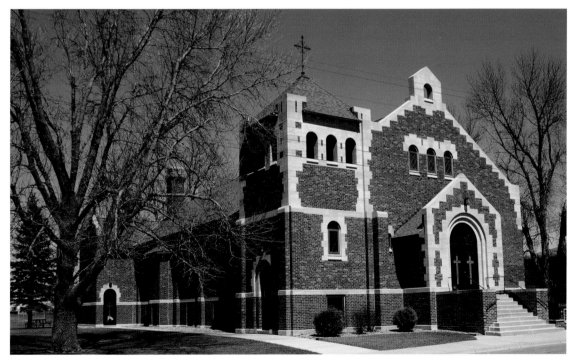

In 1907 the Minneapolis St. Paul and Sault St. Marie Railroad laid tracks through the area bypassing Meire Grove by two miles. However, a freight station was built along the line at Greenwald, contributing greatly to the growth of the town. Soon the residents began to feel that they should have their own parish, despite the fact that Greenwald was only two miles away from Meire Grove. The opportunity came in 1923 when the church at Meire Grove burned to the ground. A group from Greenwald approached the pastor at Meire Grove and offered to help financially with the church rebuilding there under the condition that they could start their own parish. Soon after, land was donated in Greenwald for a church, and on June 8, 1924, the first mass was held in the new basement church. This structure was used until 1942 when money had been raised for the present church which was built over the basement.

## ARCHITECTURAL DESCRIPTION

The Church of Saint Andrew is a rare example in the Upper Midwest of Spanish-influenced Southwestern American religious architecture, which this church draws from. It also represents the transition period in Stearns County between the early Gothic-Romanesque style and the Post World War II appearance of Modern architecture. This time frame is marked by various eclectic architectural expressions that frequently appear while a culture searches for the next style to come forth.

On the exterior, Saint Andrew's distinguishing architectural characteristics are the moderate slope of its gable roof, given emphasis with its stepped sandstone parapet blocks reaching to the ridge, which projects an upright slab rising above the parapet. The slab is shaped with vertical sides and a gable form at its top that surrounds an arch open to the sky—a feature common to the Southwest Mission style. On the left side of the façade, a rectangular bell enclosure contains a three-part series of simple vertical arch-shaped openings, whose sandstone facing is seamlessly continuous with the stone edging that outlines the façade and its entrance. A small wrought-iron decorative cross appears on top of the shallow pitched hip roof of the bell enclosure. The reddish orange-tinged brick on the exterior walls provide an appropriate complement to the sandstone's ever so faint orange traces within its predominate light brown-beige tone. Overall, the influence of the Southwest Mission Style is readily apparent, while guiding Saint Andrew's distinct architectural identity.

As might be expected, the Southwest Mission Style follows into the interior. Exposed wood glue-laminated beams in dark-brown varnish, support longitudinally running wood purlins, also in dark-brown finish, which in turn support nave ceiling/roof framing. What little other wood trim this interior possesses is likewise dark brown, which renders dramatic contrast to the expanses of white plaster recalling the Southwest Mission theme. Here at Saint Andrew, that white plaster combines Modern with Mission, as both architectural styles favor unadorned major interior surfaces with simple smooth corners and openings.

Decorative detail at Saint Andrews has limited but effective use. Stenciling forms a band around the outer curve of the arch leading to the sanctuary, and the back altar against the rear wall features richly carved detail in a three-part panel holding a crucifix in the center. Likewise, side altars of diminutive scale on both sides of the arched opening repeat the tight embellishments that surround the featured statuary.

The architecture of the Church of Saint Andrew is a successful adaptation of a distinct ethnic-based architectural style, which, in commercial uses, frequently resort to copying the conspicuous. Here, both inside and out, design models southwestern expression, achieving an intimate sense of scale and a simple balance of architectural elements that guide worship.

## KIMBALL

# Church of St. Anne

Architect: Thomas Carmody, Bloomington, Minnesota
Church renovation: Pauly, Olsen, architects ; St. Cloud
Contractor: Conlon Construction, St. Cloud
1964–1979

### PARISH HISTORY

The first Catholic parish in the Kimball area was located two miles east of the present town and was established in 1873. In the same year, a log church was built on a site donated by one of the parishioners and was used until 1894 when a tornado destroyed it. A second church was never rebuilt at this site. Instead the families attended church in the nearby towns of Watkins and Marty.

It wasn't until the town of Kimball began to grow in the early decades of the twentieth century that plans were made to re-establish a parish there. In 1919 permission was given by the bishop, and the first masses were held in the village hall by the pastor from nearby Luxemburg. In 1920 a basement

church was built, but further plans to erect a larger space for worship were delayed due to the Depression. Finally, in 1948, a social hall was built adjacent to the basement church, which provided much needed space for the congregation which was then beginning to grow. As with many parishes at this time, instead of building a separate church, Kimball embarked on the construction of a parish complex consisting of a school as well as worship space. This project was completed in 1964, but due to the shortage of teaching nuns, the school was closed in 1970. In 1979 the gymnasium of the school was converted into the permanent church and is still in use today.

## ARCHITECTURAL DESCRIPTION

The Church of Saint Anne's shallow-pitched roof can be seen stepped back from the one level multi-use structure of which the church is part. A flat-roofed canopy projecting from the main façade of the building serves as entrance to the worship space. Inside, a large entrance that is part of a corridor leads to a space that was a former gymnasium later converted to a nave for church ceremonies. An improvised bulkhead suspended from the steel web-joist ceiling structure separates the functional nave space from an unused area behind.

This improvised space follows the altar on a platform thrust outward from the rear wall and into the seating area. This plan is similar to new churches built during this time period, with pews arranged around the three sides of the altar platform. The wall behind the altar provides an interesting graphic artful composition of cross-shaped horizontal and vertical pairs of lines incised into the wall surface, with an attached modern styled crucifix. The altar table and associated furniture are of modern design, and built by a local parishioner.

In the 1960s and later, parishes often planned these multi-use facilities in staged construction that, by necessity, corresponded to staged fund raising. The demographics of growth in the Catholic population during this time produced the need for additional parochial grade schools. Moreover, emerging parish needs for social facilities that melded with religious life were met with modern architecture's one-level building types that emphasized flexible space planning to accommodate change. The strategy for parish councils was to build a gymnasium for school use that could also function on a temporary basis for religious services, and later build a definitive church space designed specifically for that use. Occasionally, however, parish growth abated, and these gymnasiums continued to serve the exercise of religion.

PAYNESVILLE

# Church of St. Louis

Architect:Louis Pinnault, St. Cloud
Builder: Boehl Construction, Paynesville
Additions and Renovations: Station 19 Architects,
Winkelman Construction, St. Cloud
1959–1988

## PARISH HISTORY

The first Catholic church in Paynesville came about in an unusual manner. An advertisement in the local newspaper in 1898 asked those Catholics in the area who were interested in starting a church to meet at an appointed time and place to formulate plans. As a result of this meeting, a parish was incorporated and a

small sum of money was raised. The method of naming the church was also quite unique. The earliest Catholic settlers in the area were Irish and French, and they decided that whoever could raise the most money for the church would have the privilege of naming it. Each vote was worth ten cents. The French won; thus the church was named St. Louis. Lots were purchased, and the first church, a converted commercial building, was moved to the site.

At a meeting in 1913, the parish approved the construction of a new church which was completed in the same year. This wood-framed structure served the parish until 1960 when a new parish complex was completed. Extensive additions and renovation to the complex were undertaken in 1988, culminating in the remodeling of the worship space. A notable feature of the interior are the large stained-glass windows designed by local art teacher Marv Fasen and built by Terhaar Studios in Cold Spring.

## ARCHITECTURAL DESCRIPTION

The Church of Saint Louis's religious spaces, built in 1959, adhered to post-World-War-II architectural direction that favored simple brick walls of undifferentiated brickwork, covered by exposed wood trusses that directly step in time with modern architecture's dictum "form follows function," visible for all to see. This visual articulation substitutes for ornamental arrays of late nineteenth- and early twentieth-century churches. Its pre-Vatican II floor plan fol-

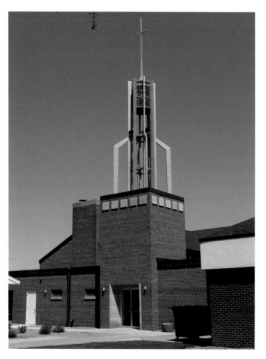

lows the basilica plan with the altar reposed and the end of the nave. A 1988 remodeling and expansion of the overall facility added a large spacious entry to the south side of the east-west-oriented nave. The addition roof trusses deftly integrate with the main nave trusswork, giving the space beneath the opportunity to re-orient to former east-west axis to north-south, placing the altar platform at mid-point of the north wall, allowing an artful terminus to the new entry and extended nave. These two nave sections achieve a sense of unity with the addition stained-glass windows using bright hues of red, blues, and orange-yellows set in angular forms that relate to the same color palette with its curved shapes of the original 1959 structure.

## St. Cloud

# Christ Church

Architect: Eugene Freerks
1964

### Parish History

Christ Church is located on the northeast edge of the campus of St. Cloud State University, and had its beginnings as a Newman Center for the students at the university. In 1956 the diocese purchased a house where the present building stands which contained clubrooms, the chaplain's residence, as well

as space for a chapel. The Catholic community at the college continued to grow, and by the early 1960s it was apparent that more space was needed for the ministry. Through the New Horizons Campaign of the diocese, a large sum was designated for a new building. This impressive structure contained, in addition to the chapel, classrooms, a student lounge, and offices. Completed in 1964, it was the first church in the St. Cloud Diocese to be built in accordance with the norms set by Vatican II. The church continued to serve only the students and staff of the university until 1972 when its status was changed to that of a personal parish.

## ARCHITECTURAL DESCRIPTION

Freerks Speryl and Flynn Architects' design for this chapel building took on several contemporary architectural themes of the day and skillfully modeled them into a coherent structure. The flat roof is constructed of cast-in-place concrete deep beams. A series of brick exterior wall panels are separated by narrow top-to-bottom slits spaced in accordance with the concrete structural framework. Exposed brick interior walls and cast-in-place concrete surfaces reveal the imprint of boards used as forms for the concrete pouring process.

Contemporary (sometimes called "modern") architecture often establishes main entrances asymmetrically from the building's façade, and the Newman Center Chapel main eight-foot-high doors are set at the corner of the building close to the sidewalk. Inside the vestibule space, a low ceiling constructed of poured concrete has a coffered pattern. Here, the architects balanced the boldness of the unfinished concrete's strong coffers and a low light level with the dramatic strong daylight pouring through open cells of the coffers and the skylights above them, giving prominence to the baptismal font centered in the space. This striking contrast of varying strengths of light playing in and around overt geometry has been emblematic in contemporary architecture.

The architects also employed contemporary architecture's favor of abandoning aligning floor plans along a linear axis, which was invariably the design principle throughout the centuries of traditional architecture. At Newman, entry to the chapel nave space is located to the left of the vestibule. The interior presents a slightly rectangular uninterrupted open space, given form by means of the poured concrete coffered ceiling with three open coffers topped by skylights set over the altar platform. The design follows traditional architecture's placement of windows along the length of side walls. But instead of stained-glass windows, tall and narrow plain glazed strips fit into insets in the masonry walls.

The table-shaped altar stands well apart from the unadorned wall behind, lending the minimalism in response to Catholicism's new spirit of the 1960s.

The St. Paul architectural firm of Freerks, Speryl, and Flynn received an honor award for the Newman Center Chapel from the Minnesota Chapter of the American Institute of Architects shortly after the building's completion.

# St. Cloud

# Church of St. Anthony

Architects: Grooters, Leapaldt, Tideman, St.Cloud
Builder: Donlar Construction, St. Cloud
2000

## Parish History

The city of St. Cloud experienced rapid growth after the turn of the twentieth century, and this growth resulted in the need for new parishes. The parish of St. Anthony was established in 1920 to accommodate the growth on the west end of St. Cloud and quickly grew to be among the largest parishes in the diocese. Their first church was a one-story wood structure completed in December of 1920. In 1921 a school was started with an opening enrollment of 175 students, and was soon at capacity, necessitating using the church for additional classrooms. In 1922 a basement church was built. In the ensuing years additions were made to the school as enrollment continued to increase. Although there was talk of building a separate church, the parish decided to use its resources in the education of its children. In 1998 plans were started for the present church located across the street from the rest of the parish complex. It was dedicated in 2000.

## Architectural Description

The dominant character of the Church of Saint Anthony is its architectural assemblage of forms across its site, with plain-faced masonry and metal-clad walls in beige tones, stepping in and out from each other, some at angles. The main entry features three tall arched openings containing glass-paneled doors and windows. The flat roof of the entry is flanked by

square towers rising above the entry with shallow gable tops that subtly recall the twin bell towers of Gothic-Romanesque traditional churches. Within the building complex, the nave extends upward with its slightly pitched roof.

Inside the entry is a high ceiling with a two-sided balcony that overlooks the entry windows and the nave beyond the entry. In the nave, the altar's location on its wide platform backs a wide wall in a way that sets the altar to face outward into two wide and relatively shallow seating areas at angles to each other. On the wall is a large sculptural Christ figure with outstretched arms. A large domed skylight above the altar provides a dramatic light source to the altar. This irregular-shaped floor layout brings the parishioners into a closer relationship with the priest and attending celebrants, showing how Vatican II influenced Saint Anthony's design with the first strokes of the architect's pencil. Its architecture represents the transition from the traditional rectangular long nave with the altar at one end that served religious services for centuries to the 1960s era that reoriented how mass was celebrated. In another transitional sense, the ornamentation that characterized the interiors of traditional churches that visually reinforced structural forms is no longer in service, as modern architecture uses geometry, proportion, and materials' texture as elements in their own right to define aesthetic form.

## St. Cloud
# Church of the Holy Spirit

Architects: Yeater,Hennings, Ruff, Schultz, and Rokke
Builder: Gohman Construction, St. Joseph
1995

### Parish History

Holy Spirit is one of several parishes that came about as a result of rapid population growth in St. Cloud in the 1940s. Until that time, there were three Catholic churches in the downtown area: St. Mary's Cathedral, Holy Angels, and St. John's Cantius. St. Anthony's had been established in 1920

to accommodate growth on the west side of the city. As the city began to grow to the south, the diocese began to make plans for an additional parish. In 1947, the pastor at St. Mary's began setting aside a portion of the weekly offerings for a future parish. In the following years the Christian Mothers organization was split so that those members living in the south side of the city held their own meetings. Next, St. Mary's members living within the boundaries of the proposed new parish began to worship as a group in the crypt chapel in the lower level of St. Mary's Cathedral. After a further period of fund raising, a school was built on the property purchased for the parish, and the first services were held in the gymnasium on Christmas Day 1953. A separate worship space was built within the school complex in 1957.

The new parish experienced continued growth as the city expanded southward over the next thirty years. In the early 1990s plans were initiated for a new church to be located closer to the southern edge of the city. The first mass in the new facility was held on Christmas Eve in 1995.

## ARCHITECTURAL DESCRIPTION

The architecture of the Church of the Holy Spirit represents a return to tradition, not in the sense of the Gothic-Romanesque ecclesiastic citadels in the prairies of Stearns County, but the recall of uncomplicated gable-roofed structures typically built for secular uses. The flat-roofed off-set walls in abstract geometry of modernism had long run its course, and the Holy Spirit congregation evidently sought the familiarity of simple gables and roof pitches, common siding and trim materials, along with a modestly-scaled steeple. A series of dormers give rhythm to the church's long walls and lend prominence to the large-sized arched stained glass-windows encased within them. Holy Spirit's sizeable main entry straddles the main nave or worship space and the fellowship section.

The church's interior follows the exterior's nondependence on ornament. Nonetheless, the warm range of beiges and browns, combined with the neutral grays of floor coverings, offer a welcoming sense, which enhances the function of the entry's orientation to the fellowship space. The worship space is covered with a semi-barrel vault ceiling, which flows in small amounts into the ceiling shapes of side gables. Laminated white-painted columns set out slightly from the side walls curve into ceiling beams. With gray carpet, clear-varnished wood trim, and medium-dark varnished pews, the interior gives a quiet sense that serves its religious purpose. This quietude, however, gives the trickling sound of the baptismal fountain a clear aural sensation that becomes swallowed into the silence of the greater space.

ST. CLOUD

# Church of St. Michael

Architect: Leo Buettner, St. Cloud
Builder: Buettner Construction, St. Cloud
Addition: Gohman Construction, St. Joseph
1970–1996

## PARISH HISTORY

St. Michael's is the youngest parish in Stearns County, established in 1969 to serve the fast-growing area on the northwest side of the city. Its church was

the first built in the St. Cloud Diocese following Vatican II. The parish was named in honor of the patron saint of Michael Kraemer on whose land the church was built. From its inception as a parish on July 1, 1969, until the new church was completed, members attended Sunday mass at a local theater. Many of the original parishioners recall that before each Sunday service, a group of volunteers arrived early to sweep up the popcorn from the previous night's movie. From the 200 families at its inception, the parish has grown to over 3,000 members. A building addition completed in 1996, added a parish center, offices, and religious education classrooms.

## ARCHITECTURAL DESCRIPTION

In the mid 1950s, as the Catholic population experienced significant increases, religious facilities planning often envisioned a multi-use one-story building, with a worship space joined by a gathering area, and a church space. The Church of Saint Michael is such an example. The identifying church element is a large white stucco gable shape projecting upward from the one-story massing of the building complex. In these post-war churches, the main entrance brought parishioners into a gathering space, much larger and more multi-functional than the centuries-old vestibule. In contrast to the vestibule, the gathering space is spacious and is served amply with sunlight by means of large windows. This space would seem to have a somewhat secular character, but a large cross in a circle shape embedded in the ceiling informs visitors and parishioners as to the purpose of the overall facility. Curved walls and granite facing material enrich the space.

The nave, entered through the gathering space, presents two seating areas extending at angles from the altar area. The asymmetrical architectural plan becomes defined by three large upward sloping beams supporting roof structure that converge over the altar under a large skylight. A hexagonal-shaped beam is suspended from the converging beam feature. The architectural intention here is to form an unorthodox and contemporary religious space by means of abstract structural geometry that lead the eyes upward to the circle of light representing the beyond and the realm of the spirit.

## St. Cloud

# Church of St. Paul

Architect: Louis Pinnault, St. Cloud
Builder: Wahl Construction, St. Cloud
1960

### PARISH HISTORY

As the population of St. Cloud grew in the late 1940s, the need to establish additional parishes was recognized by the diocese. A census was taken in the northern part of the city to determine the number of Catholics there and to gauge interest in starting a new parish. With sufficient numbers assured, a new parish, named St. Paul's, was formed in 1946. Building of the first parish facilities started immediately consisting of a school with the church in the basement, It was completed in 1948. Continued growth of the parish resulted in the need for a larger worship space, and in 1960 construction began on the present church. St. Paul's is the largest of the Catholic churches in St. Cloud, except for St. Mary's Cathedral. It measures seventy-five by 146 feet and seats 900 people.

### ARCHITECTURAL DESCRIPTION

The architectural design of the Church of Saint Paul combines modern lines with traditional forms. This can be readily seen in the church's façade, with

clean planes of brick walls and flat marble features unbroken by ornament. A two-story-high brick gable element centers in the façade. Stepping out from the façade is a vertically oriented marble gable-shaped panel containing windows that are vaguely reminiscent of a traditional Palladian pattern.

This mix of modern and traditional design occurred with some frequency in churches

built in the 1950a and early 1960s. Architectural modernism's early appearances initially came with buildings whose owners sought signature structures —college libraries, corporate headquarters, technology research facilities, and college professors' residences—coming later to public buildings and places of worship.

The modern-traditional integration continues in the interior of Saint Paul. The nave has a feeling of open space, with low pitch ceiling beams spanning from engaged plain-faced columns at the side walls. That spacious feeling receives ambience by a sensitive palette of warm tones of beiges and brown hues in interior surface components. Brick walls have variation of beiges with pinkish tint that responds well to interior light; windows along the nave walls are monochromatic translucent glass whose pale beige hues sends ample sunlight into the Saint Paul's interior; sand-tone beams and columns blend in with these soft colors while the knotty pine wood ceiling's rich varnish delivers welcome contrast. Sand-gray floor tiles provide a neutral base. The oak pews and trim members throughout the space have a clear finish, which reveals the character of the wood grain.

All in all, the warm colors of sunlight and muted surfaces render Saint Paul's with a soft atmosphere, also a commodity with several other early modern churches built in this milieu, later to be replaced during modernism's course with hard-edged design that called for a more challenging response from the religious faithful.

## St. Cloud

# Church of St. Peter

Architect: Louis Pinnault, St. Cloud
Builder: Wahl Construction, St. Cloud
1997 addition and remodeling
1958–1997

## Parish History

The growth and expansion of the city of St. Cloud in the years following World War II necessitated the formation of three new Catholic parishes in a five-year period. St. Peter's was established in 1947 to serve people in the northwest part of St. Cloud. The first church was a quonset building, completed in the summer of 1948. The parish grew quickly, and it became a priority of the parishioners to build an elementary school for its youth. The school was completed in 1954, and by 1958, an addition was needed. At this time, the gymnasium of the original school was remodeled for use as a new church.

In 1997 St. Peter's built a new parish center, and at the same time, did a complete remodeling of the church. During construction, church services were held in the quonset that had been the original church fifty years earlier.

## Architectural Description

The Church of Saint Peter is integrated within the parish school and multi-use facilities and has no stand-apart presence as an architecturally identifiable link. The worship space stands behind a one-story brick flat-roofed commons area and entry relating to school functions and is entered through a hallway. The nave is a long and somewhat low-pitched ceilinged space. Piers in the side walls curve upward as they reach the top of the walls where the sloped ceiling begins, becoming continuous with ceiling beam members. The side walls of the nave are brick in the lower surface, transitioning into exposed concrete block. Rows of canister lighting fixtures give simple accent to the ceiling.

211

The sanctuary is a continuation of the nave space, with a simple altar table facing the seating. As in many other churches built in the early modern style, wood trim throughout the space is finished with clear varnish.

As a multi-use building, the interior of Saint Peter fits well with related interior functions, and on the exterior, the gable roof ascends modestly above the surrounding one-story flat roof, giving just enough visibility.

ST. FRANCIS

# Church of St. Francis
Architects: Traynor, Hermanson, St. Cloud
1954

## PARISH HISTORY

This rural parish on the northern edge of Stearns County was formed in 1914 by a small group of area residents who formerly attended church in the nearby towns of St. Rosa, Freeport, and St. Anthony. There were those who thought that an additional parish was not really needed because of the proximity to the

other towns. In fact, Bishop Trobec did not appoint a pastor for the parish until 1915 in spite of the fact that a church had already been built. The 1915 wood-frame church was used until 1954 when a new structure was built. The old church was moved to Upsala in Morrison County where a new parish had been started and is still in use.

## ARCHITECTURAL FEATURES

The Church of Saint Francis exhibits its 1954 date of construction with an architectural design that came at the beginning of the Modern Architectural movement in America. Exterior features of the brick structure show flatness of wall surfaces free of detail, shaped within crisp corners to allow major forms to express themselves in architectural boldness—yet with uncomplicated composure. Most prominent is the bell tower—a rectangular form rising straight up from the ground, jutting out and slightly stepping back from the left side corner of the facade, its flat top several feet above the nave ridge line. The grille panels in the upper part of the bell tower shaft reflect modern architecture's method of designing functional elements that contribute to the building aesthetic. In like manner, the canopy over the entrance contains the basic functional elements for its purpose, as does the thin edges of the roof cornice. The lines of modernism however, work with this place of worship's holdover of traditional elements. The steep gabled roof, the façade located on the narrow part of the building's rectangular form, and the side wall piers separating windows have been the basis of the centuries-old basilica design. The Church of Saint Francis signals transition in architecture's past towards its future.

The traditional basilica template remains at work in Saint Francis's interior, while modernism shapes architectural design. The rectangular nave with its rows of pews leading to the sanctuary and choir loft above the narthex, accords traditional template. Modern design's practice of form and function occurs here, with exposed laminated wood beams supporting the church's roof, large three-unit white-trimmed window sets in square profile instead of vertical orientation, and basic interior white wall surfaces not dependent on decorative elements. The minimal form of the altar table stands in front of a wood paneled back altar screen at the rear wall. Simple three-part panels are minimally articulated with vertical strips; the center panel is highest of the three, with darker varnish, holds a crucifix.

Often, architectural design becomes individually special by seemingly minor elements that grace the total aesthetic. The Church of Saint Francis accomplishes this with its set of four very tall and narrow stained glass windows in the east wall upper façade whose glass segments give many-colored brilliance to the entire nave when seen from the interior. These stained glass

windows exhibit a fragmental semi-abstract composition depicting various musical instruments, with several shades of gray interspersed with the predominate reds, blues, and greens. In bright morning sunlight, the traditional rose window's declaration of glory comes forth in a much different and beautiful expression.

## St. Martin
# Church of St. Martin
Architect: Smith and Ward, Winona
Builder: Gohman Construction, St. Joseph
1969

### Parish History

The parish in St. Martin is one of oldest in Stearns County, dating back to 1858 when Benedictine missionary priest Father Clement Staub visited the area on foot to say mass at Ley's Settlement, named for Henry Ley, one of its earliest inhabitants. Father Staub was also credited with giving the town its present name and picking the location for its first church. The rapid growth in

the population of the area necessitated two additions to the original structure within the first twenty years of its construction in 1861. By the mid 1880s, plans were being made for an even bigger church. This structure, measuring fifty by 140 feet was completed in 1886. The whole parish was involved in the project from digging the basement to hauling in the brick from Cold Spring.

The parish has always been the social hub of the community, and in 1936 a social hall was built, which was remodeled and enlarged in 1980. The parish has been served by Benedictine priests since its founding 150 years ago. Over this time, the people of St. Martin have always been known for their tremendous devotion to their faith, witnessed by the fact that over 100 of its members have entered the religious life, the largest of any parish in the Diocese of St. Cloud.

By the 1960s it was clear that the 1885 church was no longer structurally sound, and planning began for the present church. The old church was torn down in 1969, and services were held in the parish hall until the new church was completed in 1970. The new church is circular, and at ninety feet in diameter, seats 600. The exterior is faced with Winona stone. Near the entrance a steel and concrete steeple holds the bells from the original church. Of interest in the interior are twenty-two stained glass windows portraying the story of the Redemption.

## ARCHITECTURAL DESCRIPTION

The Church of Saint Martin is a round church, the only such religious structure in the county. Throughout the whole of architectural history (and pre-history dwellings and religious sites), architecture has favored the rectangular, but has accommodated circular places of worship. Early Christian church design developed the basilica type of floor plan, and its rectangular variations dominated church architecture into the mid-period of the twentieth century. By then, Modernism-practicing architects looked at many ways to upset traditional design, so a round church became an idea to attempt.

With this church, the bell tower became replaced with what could be called a free-standing sculpture made from two pre-cast plank sections raised upright, with various rectangular openings cut into each member, and a vertical array of bells suspended between the planks. The church itself presents its round shape to the street, with a flat roof, topped by a tiny spire and edged by a wide white band. Rough-surfaced stone in random coursing covers the walls, and a somewhat wide series of doors within an inset band denotes the entrance.

Passing through the low-ceilinged vestibule, splayed walls guide the footsteps as well as the eyes toward the nave's well-proportioned roundness. Immediately in view—an array of squarish skylights above give concentrated pockets of brightness to the interior, randomly-placed among a scattering of recessed ceiling lights, in which light sources lend lightness to the gently curved ceiling in a low rise above the floor. The encircling walls feature a series of vertical narrow slits with stained glass windows effusing bright abstract shapes with colors of greens, yellows, and families of reds and blues.

The 1969 date of construction indicates the Church of Saint Martin took place after Vatican II, so the altar platform extending from the wall

behind it, with pews radiating outward in segmental sections serve to obey Vatican II's mission to draw priest and co-celebrants in close union with the faithful. Perhaps most important, the floor plan within the circle achieves efficiency of usable space with its intended purpose, thus adhering to the modernism tenet of form following function.

The modern architecture of Saint Martin bears an interesting contrast to the preceding Gothic-Romanesque style, in which the aesthetic experience of traditional church architecture found fulfillment in the hierarchy of detail observed in sequences, in which the lingering eye would engage deeper into extended interaction, which rendered enrichment and enjoyment. By contrast, many examples of modern architecture depend on simplicity to offer a one-idea concept, often leading to a "Is that all there is?" question.

However, Saint Martin's simplicity of form engenders an everything-seen-at-once sensation that yields a delightful aesthetic response, not unlike the immediacy of seeing the purity of a pearl in an oyster shell.

## SARTELL

# Church of
# St. Francis Xavier

Architects: Pauly ,Olsen and Associates, St. Cloud
Builder: David Guggenberger, General Contractor,
Jerry Kedrowski, Construction
1979

### PARISH HISTORY

St. Francis Xavier parish, established in 1948, is relatively new in comparison to those in the rest of Stearns County. Like several parishes in St. Cloud, it came about as the result of rapid population growth in the area in the 1940s.

The city of Sartell, lying along the Mississippi River north of St. Cloud, was incorporated in 1907, although settlement in the area had occurred as early as the 1850s. The town was named for Joseph Sartell, one of the earliest inhabitants. The construction of a dam across the river in 1905 and the completion of a paper mill at the site were the main factors in the growth that was to take place in the following decades. Many of the early residents were New Englanders, and the first church in town was Presbyterian, built in 1908. The Catholics in the area attended church in St. Cloud and Sauk Rapids.

By 1940 there was need for a parish to serve the increasing number of Catholics in Sartell. In that year, the pastor at Sauk Rapids began holding services in the City Hall. In 1948 the parish was officially established and named St. Francis Xavier, in honor of Father Pierz's patron saint. With 500 members at its inception, one of the first tasks was to build a church, and in 1949 a 124-by-forty-four-foot structure, seating 300, had been completed.

Father Edward Ramacher was named the first resident pastor at St. Francis, and immediately made plans to bring the various groups within the parish together and to set common goals for the future. He established a parish advisory council made up of representatives from business, farming, the

retired. Father Ramacher was probably best remembered for is efforts to provide social and recreational activities for the youth of the community. A large
recreational facility called Sunset Lodge was built on church property becoming the site of various plays and pageants for community members.

The parish continued to grow, and in 1980 the present church was
completed. In 2000 a gathering space was added as well as remodeling of the
adjacent elementary school.

## ARCHITECTURAL DESCRIPTION

The Church of Saint Francis Xavier is part of an extensive one-level brick-
faced building providing for multiple religious uses, situated in a campus setting with several parish buildings. The low-rise roof of the church provides
modest visibility from the exterior. A shallow gable roof extends outward from
the building entrance, leading to a wide vestibule and into a large multi-pur-
pose space. The walls are built with burnished-faced concrete block, each
unit incised in the center vertically to form eight-inch-by-eight-inch modules,
giving background articulation to the space. A large circle form set several
inches from the ceiling symbolizes the space's purpose of gathering.

A series of doors lead to the nave. Inside, laminated wood structural
beam/column members, which stand against sand-toned brick nave walls, tip
outward into low-pitch beams to support the roof. Ceiling plaster provides infill
between the beams. Recessed plaster ceiling slots extend alongside each beam
face, from the walls to a slightly-dropped center ceiling panel that runs under
the ceiling ridge line. These recessed slots allow considerable visibility to the
beam faces, which create strong articulation to the expansive ceiling. The
beams continue with thin exposure under the face of the center ceiling panel.

A granite stone-faced wall composed of long modular units with varying color ranges of grays and reds, gives focus to the sanctuary area. On each
end of the granite wall are long vertical stained-glass slits, which separate this
wall section from the typical rear nave wall. A multi-angled platform extends
forward from the granite wall to form the altar area. Pews in slanted rows align
symmetrically around the three sides of the altar platform.

The architectural components of Saint Francis' interior—wide uninterrupted space, low-pitched ceiling demarcated with wood structure inter-
rupted by an offset plane of ceiling, light-colored brick walls, angular lines
that enhance architectural composition—are attributes used by Frank Lloyd
Wright who influenced American architecture more than any other architect.
Nonetheless, that influence brought forth many buildings with well-inten-
tioned efforts but with questionable results. The Church of Saint Francis
Xavier is a successful and pleasant outcome of the Wrightian legacy.

# Glossary

Ambulatory—aisle around the apse of the church, usually a space between a curved series of columns and the rear exterior wall of the apse

Apse—part of the church behind the altar which projects from the wall, often semi- circular or polygonal in shape

Arcade—a series of arches with supporting columns, sometimes closed at the back

Ashlar –squared building stones, usually hewn from rough-faced stones

Baldachin—a canopy, usually over the altar and supported by columns

Baroque—an architectural style common in Europe in the 17th and 18th centuries characterized by an abundance of ornamentation

Barrel vault—a semicircular ceiling structure reaching wall to wall over the nave

Basilica design—church which follows the shape of early Roman structures: rectangular in shape with a low pitched roof

Bay—the space between supporting columns of the walls. Churches and other buildings sometimes are measured descriptively by their number of bays.

Bead molding, beaded joint—a typically narrow convex rounded strip protruding or embedded in a flat surface plane that lends a linear profile; a beaded joint in masonry with a convex rounded shape projecting from the mortar bed

Bond—although typically referring to a solid connection of two materials, in brick or blockwork, bond describes masonry configurations as laid in coursing (see coursing below).

Belfry—the part of the church steeple encasing the bells

Bracket—An overhanging member projecting from a wall acting to support the weight or structure, such as a beam or lower section of an arch. In a church, brackets typically have ornamented surfaces.

Buttress—A projecting masonry structure built against a wall and used to resist the outward thrust of an arch

Came—a slender flexible rod of lead, often with grooves, used in stained glass or leaded glass fabrication, that holds individual glass pieces in place

Campanile—a bell tower which is detached, or sometimes semi-detached, from the church; common in Italian church architecture

Canopy—a small, usually ornamented roof structure over a niche or statues within a church

Clerestory—the part of the wall of a church that rises above the aisles, usually punctuated with windows to let in light

Colonnade—a row of columns, usually covered with a roof, projecting from the building

Corbelling—courses of stones or bricks, with each row projecting out slightly from the row below it, typically built at the top of a masonry wall

Corinthian capital—the ornamental cap of a column with florid elements; this style has its origins in Greek and Roman architecture

Cornice—a molded, decorous projection running horizontally at the meeting of the top of an exterior wall and roof, or over a door or window

Course, Coursing—a layer of masonry units in a series running horizontally and bonded with mortar, forming one of many stacked masonry layers making the wall

Cove—a concave molding at the junction of the top of a wall and soffit or ceiling

Crennelated—top of walls with alternating open spaces and raised flat-topped sections in a repeated pattern

Crown—the curved top of an arch, or any curved element

Cruciform—church designed in the shape of a cross as seen in the floor layout

Detail—parts of an overall architectural design that are identifiable elements or features

Dressed—the face of a stone given a smooth or consistent finish surface

Eclectic—used in architectural references for buildings that adopt styles of previous eras.

Entablature—the flat top of a column immediately above the capital

Façade—the front or face of a building; its design often denotes a particular architectural style

Flemish bond—masonry coursing which alternates brick lengths with brick ends in a continuing pattern, staggered with brick coursing above and below

Gable—the triangular portion at the ends of a building having sloped roofs, from the eaves to the top of the roof

Gambrel—Roof type with two pitches on each side, often used for barn roof construction

Gothic/ Gothic Revival—a style of architecture prevalent in Europe from the 12th through 16th centuries; it was characterized by pointed arches, steep roofs, ribbed vaults and an emphasis on height. The style was revived (as Gothic Revival) in Europe and the United States in the latter half of the 19th century, finding architectural expression in academic buildings, residences and churches. Gothic Revival churches intended to reproduce the decorative aspects of Gothic with pronounced emphasis on verticality, with architectural features such as tracery details applied as surface treatment.

Glory—the luminous halo encircling the head of a sacred person; the luminous emanation radiating from the whole figure

Hammer beam roof vaulting—a central arched vault is supported on each side by lesser size half-arched vaults supported from upper nave walls.

Haunches—parts of the arch on either side of the crown

Head—Generally the top member of a structure or trim assembly, usually applied to windows and doors

Header coursing—masonry coursing using the end sections of brick laid alongside each other in a continuous course

Modillion—the ornamental brackets usually found under the Corinthian entablature on columns

Molding—surface or surfaces given various contours, linear projections or cavities in rectangular, curved, compound-curved or composite curved and rectangular profiles, usually applied to provide articulation to flat or simple curved surfaces

Muntins—thin wood bars that hold assemblies of stained glass windows in the sash

Narthex—the vestibule of the church leading to the nave

Nave—the central part of the church where the congregation is seated

Parapets—the part of the wall reaching above the roof level, usually on the façade Pediment—decoration over doors and windows, either rounded or triangular in shape

Pilaster—an upright member or column which serves to reinforce the wall; it sometimes projects from the outer wall

Polychrome—several paint colors applied to statuary or molded ornament

Purlin—a structural member connecting widely spaced principal roof beams to support common roof rafters

Quatrefoil—Rounded or leaf-like decoration in churches; in quatrefoil, there are four leaves (foils) in the pattern

Rake—a slope in a floor system, from level, occasionally used in church main worship spaces

Raked Joint—a mortar joint deeper into the mortar bed than typical joints, allowing shadows to bring a relief appearance to masonry units

Random coursing—masonry units, typically stone, of several varying dimensions, are laid in a seemingly random manner, but form overlay patterns.

Relief panel—pictures or carvings in which the main features are raised from the surface of the panel giving them a three dimensional appearance

Reredos—a screen or wooden structure behind the altar, most often made of wood and containing niches for statuary

Rib—a structural member supporting curved shapes of an arched ceiling vault, usually holding adjoining edges of vaulting

Romanesque/ Romanesque revival—a style of architecture that emerged in Western Europe in the 11th century that continued into the 12th century before the rise of Gothic architecture. Its Revival style began in Europe and the United States in the 19th century. It is characterized by heavier massing of components, rounded arches, and barrel vaulted ceilings

Rose window—a circular stained glass window filled with spoke-like tracery radiating from the center

Running bond—Most typical masonry coursing is running bond, in which lengths of identically sized brick follow one another uniformly, with successive courses staggering lengths atop each other.

Sacristy—a room adjacent to the sanctuary where the priest prepares for the mass

Sanctuary—The immediate area around the principal altar, the chancel

Spire—the upper part of the tower that tapers to a point; the steeple

Stack bond—refers to concrete block, often used in modern construction in which successive courses stack masonry blocks exactly above each other, instead of lapping the units.

Stations of the Cross—Depictions along the side walls of the nave of the passion and crucifixion of Christ. There are fourteen stations in all.

Steeple—the tower attached to the church that holds the bells

Tracery—intersecting and curvilinear rib work in the heads of stained glass windows used as decoration; can also be found in open patterns intended as ornamental detail on arches and vaults

Transept—the crosswise part of a cruciform church lying between the main part of the nave and the sanctuary

Trefoil—ornamental foliation taking the form of leaves found along wall surfaces

Tripartite—decorative features such as niches made up in a set of three

Tympanum —a recessed space on the face of the pediment, often containing carved stone or other decorative designs

Vault—an arched structure forming a ceiling or section of a ceiling; the two types commonly seen in churches are barrel vaults and ribbed vaults

Vestibule—the entrance of the church between the outer door and the door to the nave

Wainscot—A lower section of wall clad with a surface or structural material different than the wall above

# Bibliography

Chiat, Marilyn J. *America's Religious Architecture*. Washington D.C.: National Trust for Historic Preservation, 1997.

Ferguson, George. *Signs and Symbols in Christian Art*. New York: Oxford University Press, 1954.

Furlan, Reverend William P. *In Charity Unfeigned*. St. Cloud: Diocese of St. Cloud, 1952

Giedion, Sigfried. *Space, Time and Architecture*. Cambridge: Harvard University Press, 1959.

Hamlin, Talbot. *Architecture Through the Ages*. New York: G. P. Putnam and Sons, 1940.

Lathrop, Alan. *Churches of Minnesota; An Illustrated Guide*. Minneapolis: University of Minnesota Press, 2003.

Lyndon, Donlyn and Moore, Charles. *Chambers for a Memory Palace*. Cambridge: MIT Press, 1996.

Mitchell, William Bell. *History of Stearns County*. Chicago: H.C.Cooper, Jr., 1915.

Ohman, Doug and Hassler, Jon. *Churches of Minnesota*. St. Paul: Minnesota Historical Society Press, 2006.

von Simson, Otto. *The Gothic Cathedral*. New York: Harper Torchbooks, 1956.

Rykwert, Joseph. *Church Building*. London: Hawthorn Books, 1966

Yzermans, Reverend Vincent A. *The Spirit in Central Minnesota*. St. Cloud: The Diocese of St. Cloud, 1989.

## OTHER RESOURCES

Chiat, Marilyn. Interviews and research notes

Ferguson, Robert. Interviews

Granger, Susan. National Register Continuation Form for Church of St. Mary, Melrose, MN

Lathrop, Alan. Interview

Mack, Robert, FAIA. Ongoing conversations while running.

Stearns History Museum, St. Cloud, MN. Subject Files

University of Houston: Engines of our Ingenuity, Episode no. 986, Radio Station KUHF FM, Houston, Texas.

# Acknowledgements

I wish to thank the following people for their assistance in my writing efforts: Robert Ferguson, whose prodigious knowledge of European religious architecture has been especially rewarding; Barb Haselbeck, for her early editing and her help in guiding my writing to be concise in shaping meaning; William Morgan, who convinced us that this book should be written and his wisdom that helped in many ways; Cecelia and Corinne Dwyer of North Star Press, for their expert guidance and inspiration in the process of putting our book together; Marilyn Chiat, whose religious architectural knowledge, sharing of her research and her review of our writing has been very helpful; Alan Lathrop, who reviewed our efforts in its early stages; Christine Boulware, whose knowledge of ethnic architectural expression was very helpful; Dale Mulfinger, for guiding the landscape of book writing; Bob Mack, for his astute architectural expertise; Susan Granger, for sharing her background of Stearns County architecture. I am grateful to my wife Sally for her insights, guidance and understanding.

Robert Roscoe
Minneapolis
April, 2009


During the research phase of this book, I spent a great deal of time at the Stearns History Museum. I wish to thank the staff in the archives for their assistance, especially John Decker, Assistant Director/ Archivist. His expertise always sent me in the right direction for information. I appreciate greatly the advice and encouragement given by the" Ream Team", a local writers group to which I belong. This project has taken several years to complete and "the book" has taken on a life of its own. I am especially grateful to my wife Fran for her patience and support. I have also been appreciative of all the encouragement given by my children, Christine and Michael. My brother Bill and sister Mary have always been very supportive of our endeavor.

John Roscoe
Sartell
April, 2009

# About the Authors

## JOHN ROSCOE

My writing and historical research has developed from my educational career, teaching literature and writing for the Aitkin and Albany, Minnesota school districts. My education includes a Bachelor of Science degree in Education from St. Cloud State University with a major in English as well as graduate studies at St. Cloud State and the University of Minnesota.

As a resident of Stearns County for nearly forty years, I have become keenly aware of the heritage of the majority of its residents and how that heritage has influenced its present culture. In the past several years, I have formed working relationships with historians in the Stearns County area. The research involved in writing this book has led me to an even greater appreciation of the immigrant experience and how it produced the remarkable outcomes embodied in its churches.

John Roscoe, Robert Roscoe, and Doug Ohman

## ROBERT ROSCOE

My primary work is Design for Preservation, devoted to residential renovation, with an emphasis on historic preservation. My professional experience includes 36 years of architectural office experience. My education includes a Bachelor of Arts degree in Art History, five years School of Architecture at the University of Minnesota.

My writing has been focused on architectural aspects of historic preservation-related issues. I served as editor of the Minnesota Preservationist, a publication of the Preservation Alliance of Minnesota for 14 years. I wrote a column, Endangered, for Architecture Minnesota, a publication of the Minnesota chapter of the American Institute of Architects. Currently. I am a contributing writer for the Preservation Journal of Saint Paul and the blog Building Minnesota. In addition, I am editor of the Journal of American Rocket Science, which is available through my architectural website, www.designforpreservation.com under the category "serious research."

My historic preservation experience includes serving for 21 years as Commissioner on the Minneapolis Heritage Preservation Commission. From time to time, I have given lectures on preservation architecture at the University of Minnesota School of Architecture and Landscape Architecture, the Minnesota Chapter of the Society of Architectural Historians as well as other local public forums. I have taught a course entitled Challenges in Historic Preservation in the Center for Urban and Regional Affairs at the University of Minnesota.

Through my professional practice and commitment to historic preservation, I feel I have gained insights into how the architecture is created, how its cultural influences guide the design process towards the future that eventually continues history.

## DOUG OHMAN

Doug Ohman is an acclaimed photographer with extensive experience in photography, has produced images from every county in Minnesota, many which appear in a wide array of leading publications and exhibits of historic preservation. These photographs aptly express the architectural attributes of the buildings while revealing the regional characteristics of their setting.

Doug has also produced a series of books for the Minnesota Historical Society Press, including *Barns of Minnesota, Courthouses of Minnesota, Churches of Minnesota* and others. His photographs of architectural icons lavishly illustrate each book and are accompanied by narratives by well-known Minnesota authors.